'Michael Howlett's *The Policy 1*
years of research and practice i
The bad news is that a surprisir
to deliver what it promises. Bu
practitioners are more likely to discover what works, when and for
whom – vital pre-requisites for more effective societal problem solving'.
— *Professor Andrew Jordan, University of East Anglia, UK*

'How might governments choose the most appropriate tool for achieving
desired policy goals and objectives? How might they uncover innovative
and durable solutions? Howlett's *The Policy Design Primer: Choosing the
Right Tools for the Job* provides, in one place, the critical theoretical,
conceptual and analytical tools for making informed decisions in a highly
complex and globalized world. The book is must reading for government
and bureaucratic officials seeking to manage complex problems that
often demand, and can benefit from, drawing on procedural tools that
integrate key stakeholders into public management design and practice,
and substantive instruments that can steer policy subsystems towards
meaningful results. A tour de force in its integration of conceptual
breadth, analytical scope and practical insights'.
— *Professor Benjamin Cashore, Yale University, USA*

The Policy Design Primer

The Policy Design Primer is a concise and practical introduction to the principles and elements of policy design in contemporary governance. Guiding students through the study of the instruments used by governments in carrying out their tasks, adapting to, and altering their environments, this book:

- Examines the range of substantive and procedural policy instruments that together comprise the toolbox from which governments select specific tools expected to resolve policy problems,
- Considers the principles behind the selection and use of specific types of instruments in contemporary government,
- Addresses the issues of instrument mixes and their (re)design in a discussion of the future research agenda of policy design and
- Discusses several current trends in instrument use often linked to factors such as globalization and the increasingly networked nature of modern society.

This readily digestible and informative book provides a comprehensive overview of this essential component of modern governance, featuring helpful definitions of key concepts and further reading.

This book is essential reading for all students of public policy, administration and management as well as more broadly for relevant courses in health, social welfare, environment, development and local government, in addition to those managers and practitioners involved in Executive Education and policy design work on the ground.

Michael Howlett is Burnaby Mountain Professor and Canada Research Chair (Tier 1) in the Department of Political Science at Simon Fraser University, Canada. He specializes in public policy analysis, political economy and resource and environmental policy.

Routledge Textbooks in Policy Studies

This series provides high-quality textbooks and teaching materials for upper-level courses on all aspects of public policy as well as policy analysis, design, practice and evaluation. Each text is authored or edited by a leading scholar in the field and aims both to survey established areas and present the latest thinking on emerging topics.

Analyzing Public Policy, 2nd Edition
Peter John

Public Policy and Private Interest
Ideas, Self-Interest and Ethics in Public Policy
J.A. Chandler

The Public Policy Primer, 2nd edition
Managing the Policy Process
Xun Wu, M. Ramesh, Michael Howlett and Scott A. Fritzen

Designing Public Policies, 2nd edition
Principles and Instruments
Michael Howlett

Policy Styles and Policy-Making
Exploring the Linkages
Edited by Michael Howlett and Jale Tosun

The Policy Design Primer
Choosing the Right Tools for the Job
Michael Howlett

The Policy Design Primer

Choosing the Right Tools for the Job

Michael Howlett

Routledge
Taylor & Francis Group

LONDON AND NEW YORK

First published 2019
by Routledge
2 Park Square, Milton Park, Abingdon, Oxon OX14 4RN

and by Routledge
52 Vanderbilt Avenue, New York, NY 10017

Routledge is an imprint of the Taylor & Francis Group, an informa business

British Library Cataloguing-in-Publication Data
A catalogue record for this book is available from the British Library

Library of Congress Cataloging-in-Publication Data
Names: Howlett, Michael, 1955– author.
Title: The policy design primer: choosing the right tools for
the job / Michael Howlett.
Description: Abingdon, Oxon; New York, NY: Routledge, 2019. |
Series: Routledge textbooks in policy studies | Includes bibliographical
references and index.
Identifiers: LCCN 2018059423 (print) | LCCN 2019006616 (ebook) |
ISBN 9780429401046 (master ebook) | ISBN 9780429684517 (web pdf) |
ISBN 9780429684500 (ePub) | ISBN 9780429684494 (mobipocket/kindle) |
ISBN 9780367001612 (hbk: alk. paper) | ISBN 9780367001650
(pbk: alk. paper) | ISBN 9780429401046 (ebk)
Subjects: LCSH: Political planning. | Policy sciences.
Classification: LCC JF1525.P6 (ebook) | LCC JF1525.P6 H7 2019 (print) |
DDC 320.6—dc23
LC record available at https://lccn.loc.gov/2018059423

ISBN: 978-0-367-00161-2 (hbk)
ISBN: 978-0-367-00165-0 (pbk)
ISBN: 978-0-429-40104-6 (ebk)

Typeset in Bembo
by codeMantra

Contents

Figures

Tables

Preface

This book introduces students to the principles and elements of policy design in contemporary governance. It does so through the detailed study of the implementation instruments used by governments in carrying out their tasks in adapting to, and altering, their environments, and of the processes in government which lead to their selection and enactment. These tools form the basic foundation or structure upon which all policies and programmes rest. An essential component of modern governance, the range of substantive and procedural policy instruments together comprise the toolbox from which governments select specific tools expected to resolve particular kinds of policy problems. The book begins with the discussion of the definition of policy design and the principles behind the selection and use of specific types of instruments in the process of policy formulation. After setting out the details and strengths and weaknesses of different types of tools in subsequent chapters, by way of conclusion, the issue of how best to design policy programmes is addressed.

Acknowledgements

The book could not have been written without the pioneering work of the many scholars and colleagues who individually and collectively spent a great deal of time and effort developing the empirical cases and carefully building the many frameworks and models used throughout the text. A special debt is owed to Rebecca Raglon for her patience, support and encouragement.

Part I

Policy design in the modern state

1 Basic concepts and vocabulary

Transforming policy ambitions into practice is a complex process. According to Davis Bobrow's (2006) apt phrase, policy design is 'ubiquitous, necessary and difficult'. But it is also surprisingly less studied and poorly understood. Unfortunately, many efforts made by policy-makers to address policy problems still fail. But these experiences have fortunately led to a greater awareness of various obstacles that can present themselves to effective policy designs. Efforts to overcome these obstacles, in turn, gradually have fueled a better understanding of the characteristics of the policy process through which design occurs.

Policy design itself entails *the conscious and deliberate effort to define policy aims and map them instrumentally to policy tools that are expected to achieve those aims.* In this sense, policy design is a particular type of policy formulation, involving activities like collecting knowledge about the outcomes of policy instrument use on policy targets and analyzing its relevance to the creation and implementation of policies meant to attain specific policy goals and aspirations.

The tools orientation towards policy design: authoritative instrumentalism

The origins of policy design studies in the sense used in this book can be traced to the very roots of the policy sciences in the 1950s and 1960s which espoused the overall idea of affecting better outcomes of government actions through the organized application of knowledge to policy-making (Wildavsky 1979). The academic enquiry of policy design – that is, self-consciously dealing with both policy processes and substance from an instrumental perspective – emerged and flourished throughout the 1980s and 1990s (Linder and Peters 1991).

In contemporary policy studies, 'design' is associated with both the identification and analysis of policy instruments and their implementation. Policy design in this sense has a *substantive* element that comprises the technical arrangements of alternatives that could potentially resolve a policy problem at hand, and a *procedural* component linked to the processes and activities necessary to coordinate the activities of policy actors (Howlett 2011). The contemporary design orientation in policy studies involves thinking about policy design beyond individual policy tool choices to the study of combinations of substantive and procedural instruments and their interactions in sometimes very complex policy mixes. It also has focused on detailed study of the actual formulation processes involved in tool and design choices, as these mixes are created and evolve over sometimes considerable lengths of time.

This chapter provides an introduction to this body of work, setting out the basic concepts and definitions used in the field. Subsequent chapters examine the logic of policy design and the considerations and experiences which are linked to the choices of specific kinds of policy tools found in common designs.

What is public policy?

Public policies are government decisions composed of *policy goals* and *means* at different levels of abstraction (Lasswell 1951). Policy goals are the basic aims and expectations governments have in deciding to pursue (or not) some course of action, while policy means are the techniques governments use to attain those goals. Both these elements can be focused on a range of activities, from principles associated with governance arrangements such as free markets or regulation, to more concrete day-to-day administrative programme specifications having to do with topics such as the size of fines levied to discourage activities like littering or theft.

A typical policy contains some very abstract general 'aims' or goals, such as, in the cases of criminal justice or education policy, attaining a just society or an innovative one, along with a set of less abstract 'objectives' actually expected to achieve those aims such as reducing crime or providing lifelong educational opportunities to members of the public. Further, those objectives themselves must be set down as specific targets or measures which allow policy resources to be directed towards their attainment, such as reducing specific types of crimes such as autotheft or robberies to specific levels within specified periods of time or increasing post-secondary educational attendance or completion by some percentage within a set temporal period.

Similarly, the means or techniques for achieving goals run from highly abstract preferences for specific forms of policy implementation, such as a preference for the use of market, government or non-profit forms of organization in areas such as healthcare, education or crime prevention, to the more concrete level of the use of specific governing tools or mechanisms such as regulation, information campaigns, public enterprises or government subsidies to alter actor behaviour in order to promote or increase wellness, improve educational service delivery or prevent crime. And this runs even further to the most specific level of deciding or determining exactly how those tools should be 'calibrated' in order to achieve policy targets, such as providing a specific number of additional police on the streets within a specified period of time, a specific number of kindergarten teachers or a specific level of subsidy to non-profit groups to provide home nursing services.

The principle 'components' of public policies involved in any policy design, following this logic, are set out in Table 1.1.

ble 1.1 Components of public policies involved in policy design

		Policy level		
		Governance mode: high-level abstraction	*Policy regime: programme-level operationalization*	*Programme settings specific on-the-ground measures*
licy component	Policy goals	General abstract policy aims: The most general macro-level statement of government aims and ambitions in a specific policy area	Operationalizable policy objectives: The specific meso-level areas that policies are expected to address in order to achieve policy aims	Specific policy targets: The specific, on-the-ground, aims of efforts to achieve objectives and aims
	Policy means	General policy implementation preferences: The long-term preferences of government in terms of the types of organizational devices to be used in addressing policy aims	Policy tool choices: The specific types of governing instruments to be used to address programme-level objectives	Specific policy tool calibrations: The specific 'settings' of policy tools required to implement policy programmes

urce: Howlett (2009).

What is policy design?

Within the policy sciences, 'design' involves the deliberate and conscious attempt to define these policy goals and connect them in a logical or 'instrumental' fashion to policy tools thought to be able to achieve them (May, 2003). Policy design, in this sense, is a specific form of policy formulation based on the gathering of knowledge about the effects of policy tool use on policy targets and the application of that knowledge to the development and implementation of each component of a policy. It is an activity conducted by a number of policy actors in the hope of improving policy-making and policy outcomes through the accurate anticipation of the consequences of government actions.

Policy design extends to both the means or mechanisms through which goals are given effect, and to the goals themselves, since goal articulation inevitably involves considerations of feasibility, or what is practical or possible to achieve in given circumstances considering the means at hand. This is the bread-and-butter of policy analytical work undertaken by civil services, think tanks, policy institutes and policy schools which generally examine existing arrangements and propose new or revised solutions felt likely to effectively achieve policy goals.

Not all policy formulation is disinterested or includes this design orientation, however. In many situations, formulators may engage in self-interested behaviour and engage in interest-driven trade-offs or log-rolling between stakeholders or each other, or, more extremely, might engage in venal or corrupt behaviour in which personal gain is the paramount consideration in proposing and advocating for certain kinds of actions and activities. These 'non-design' situations are well known in practice but unfortunately are often ignored in studies focusing exclusively on policy designs and designing.

It is also important to note that policy-making and especially policy tool selection are highly constrained processes even when goodwill and a design orientation exists. The exact processes by which policy decisions are taken vary greatly by jurisdiction and sector and reflect the great differences and nuances that exist between different forms of government – from military regimes to liberal democracies and within each type – as well as the particular configuration of issues, actors and problems governments face in particular areas or 'sectors' of activity – such as health or education policy, industrial policy, transportation or energy policy and social policy (Howlett et al. 2009). In some circumstances, policy decisions will be more highly contingent and 'irrational' or less instrumental than others, that is, driven by situational logics and opportunism rather than careful deliberation and assessment. Such situations and possibilities must always remain at the forefront of policy design studies.

What is a policy instrument?

The policy alternatives which policy designers create are composed of different sets or combinations of policy tools, described in more detail in Chapters 3–6 of this book. Other terms have been developed in the field of policy studies to describe the same phenomenon, such as 'governing instruments', 'policy instruments' and the 'tools of government', and while these sometimes are used to refer to different things, they are more often used synonymously. These tools are the subject of deliberation and activity at all stages of the policy process and affect both the agenda-setting and policy formulation processes as well as being the subject of decision-making, policy implementation and evaluation.

Taken together, the tools of government comprise the contents of the toolbox from which decision-makers must choose in building or creating public policies. Policy design elevates the analysis and practice of these policy instrument choices to a central focus of study, making their understanding and analysis a key design concern (Salamon 1981, 2002). Instrument choice, from this perspective, in a sense, *is* public policy-making, and understanding and analyzing potential instrument choices involved in implementation activity *is* policy design.

Tool choice has both a supply and a demand aspect. Some tools may be more popular with decision-makers than others – an aversion to taxes and a preference for market solutions to governing problems witnessed in many countries in recent decades being a good example – and hence enjoy different levels of 'demand'. On the supply side, these tools rely on a set of governing resources for their effectiveness, including 'nodality' (or information), authority, treasure or the organizational resources of government (see Table 1.2) and the availability of, for example, ample treasure resources to provide subsidies to individuals or firms affects their supply and selection.

It is also important to note that tools can have both 'positive' attributes such as enhancing civil rights and democratic practices, or 'negative' ones such as favouring certain actors over others or preventing and prohibiting certain kinds of otherwise desirable activities. Thus, information-based instruments, for example, can both facilitate the provision of information as well as suppress it, and can involve the

Table 1.2 A Resource-based taxonomy of procedural and substantive policy
instruments (cells provide examples of instruments in each category)

Governing resource and target need

		Information	Authority	Treasure	Organization
Purpose of tool	**Substantive**	Public information campaign	Independent regulatory agencies	Subsidies and grants	Public enterprises
	Procedural	Official secrets acts	Administrative advisory committees	Interest group funding	Government re-organizations

Source: Adapted from Howlett (2000), based on Hood (1986).

release of misleading as well as accurate information (Goodin 1980).
In this sense it is important for designers to be aware that tools can
be 'two-edged swords' and used for both emancipatory and repressive
purposes.

What is an implementation tool?

Policy instruments appear in all stages of the policy process. Those
affecting the agenda-setting, decision-making and evaluation stages of
the policy process, such as rules and funding affecting the media, those
limiting the remit of cabinets and executives and those promoting policy
learning and lesson-drawing, are very significant and important in public
management. However, most policy designs deal with plans for implementation, and thus the key sets of policy instruments of concern to most
policy designers are those linked to policy implementation in the first
instance, and to policy formulation in the second. In the first category,
we would find examples of many well-known governing tools such as the
public enterprises and regulatory agencies which are omnipresent in government and expected to alter or affect the delivery of goods and services
to both the public and the government itself. In the second we would
find instruments such as regulatory or environmental impact appraisals or
provisions for stakeholder consultations which are designed to alter and
affect some aspect of the nature of policy deliberations and the mention,
development, consideration and assessment of alternatives.

While all of these tools are interesting and important, the role
played by implementation instruments in policy design is the central
focus of this book. They are the core tools which affect either the
content or processes of policy implementation, that is, which alter the
way goods and services are delivered to the public or the manner in
which decisions about them take place. As Linder and Peters (1984)

noted, it is critical for policy scientists and policy designers alike to understand the basic vocabulary of design which is represented by these tools. As they note, 'whether the problem is an architectural, mechanical or administrative one, the logic of design is fundamentally similar'. The idea behind all of these types of design is to 'fashion an instrument that will work in a desired manner'. Examining policy problems from a design perspective focusing on implementation tools, they argue, offers a productive way of organizing thinking and analytical efforts around them. (253).

Vedung (1997) usefully defined these instruments as *'the set of techniques by which governmental authorities wield their power in attempting to ensure support and effect social change'*. This definition can be seen to include both 'substantive' tools, those Hood (1986) defined as attempting to 'effect or detect' change in the socio-economic system, and 'procedural' tools designed to 'ensure support' for government actions.

Substantive implementation instruments can affect many aspects of production, distribution and consumption of goods and services. Production effects, for example, include determining or influencing:

1 Who produces a good or service – for example, via licencing, bureaucracy/procurement or subsidies for new start-ups.
2 The types of goods and services produced – for example, through bans or limits or encouragement.
3 The quantity of goods or services provided – for example, via subsidies or quotas.
4 The quality of goods or services produced – for example, via product standards, warranties.
5 Methods of production – for example, via environmental standards or subsidies for modernization.
6 Conditions of production – for example, via health and safety standards, employment standards acts, minimum wage laws, inspections.
7 The organization of production – for example, via unionization rules, anti-trust or anti-combines legislation, securities legislation or tax laws.

Consumption and distribution effects from substantive implementation tool deployment are also manifold. Some examples of these are:

1 Setting the prices of goods and services – such as regulated taxi fares or wartime rationing.
2 Affecting the distribution of produced goods and services – affecting the location and types of schools or hospitals, forest tenures or leases, for example.

3   Affecting the level of consumer demand for specific goods – for example, through information release, nutritional and dangerous goods labelling (cigarettes), export and import taxes and bans and similar activities.
4   Altering the level of consumer demand in general – via interest rate, monetary and fiscal policy.

Procedurally oriented implementation tools, on the other hand, affect production, consumption and distribution processes only indirectly, if at all. They instead affect the behaviour of actors involved in policy formulation and implementation. In policy-making, policy actors are arrayed in various kinds of policy communities or networks, and just as substantive implementation instruments can alter or affect the actions of citizens in the productive realm, so too can procedural implementation instruments affect and alter aspects of the policy-making behaviour of these actors. Such procedural implementation tools are an important part of government activities aimed at altering policy interaction within policy sub-systems, but, as Klijn et al. (1995) put it, they typically 'structure . . . the game without determining its outcome' (441). That is, these tools affect the manner in which implementation unfolds but without necessarily predetermining its results.

Some of the kinds of policy activities that can be affected by the use of procedural implementation tools (Goldsmith and Eggers 2004) include:

1   changing actor policy positions through subsidies, information or co-optation
2   setting down, defining or refining actor positions through formal consultation processes
3   adding actors to policy networks through the creation of interest groups or thinktanks
4   changing access rules for actors to governments and networks through altering formal or informal governing and policy-making processes
5   influencing network formation through activities such as conferencing and funding
6   promoting network self-regulation through the extension of recognition to specific processes and not others
7   modifying system-level policy parameters (e.g. levels of non-governmental organization market reliance through extension of charitable donation laws or direct government funding for interest group activities or services
8   changing evaluative criteria for assessing policy outcomes, success and failure in laws , regulations and rules
9   influencing the pay-off structure for policy actors such as interest groups by making information easier or harder to come by

10 influencing professional and other codes of conduct affecting policy
    actor behaviour in regulations on the subject
11 regulating inter-actor policy conflict through government agencies
    and tribunals in areas such as labour or human rights
12 changing policy actors' interaction procedures by altering how
    they interact with governments
13 certifying or sanctioning certain types of policy-relevant behaviour
    through its recognition and sanctification by government actors and
    rules
14 changing supervisory relations between actors by affecting the rules of
    access of certain groups and not others to government officials and actors.

Policy designs typically contain 'bundles' or 'mixes' of several procedural and substantive implementation tools and the relations between
these tools are sometimes complementary and sometimes not, a subject
of some importance in policy design to which we will return in subsequent chapters.

What isn't policy design?

As mentioned above, policy decisions can be careful and deliberate in
attempting to find the best way to resolve a problem or can be highly
contingent and driven by situational logics and political or economic
self-interest. And decisions stemming from legislative bargaining or
electoral opportunism can also be distinguished from those which
result from careful analysis and assessment in deliberative forums
created or used specifically for design purposes. In the latter situation
of well-intentioned and public-spirited actors 'policy design' implies
a knowledge-based process in which the choice of means or the tools
through which policy goals are given effect follows a logical process of
inference from known or learnt relationships between means and outcomes. Importantly, this includes designs in which means are selected
in accordance with experience and knowledge in which principles and
relationships may be incorrectly or only partially articulated or understood, the key criteria being knowledge-based deliberation in the
public interest.

  When such propitious conditions are present, purposive design activity resulting in good alternative generation and assessment is possible, is
typically the case in the modern era at most times in most governments.
Although having such deliberations does not guarantee ultimate success, the chances of successfully eliminating problems and improving
conditions are greater than when these conditions are not present. In
purely self-interested or non-evidentiary situations either poor designs

Table 1.3 Types of policy formulation spaces: situating design and non–design processes

		Level of government knowledge and other constraints	
		High	Low
Government formulation intention	More instrumental	**Capable policy design space** Relatively unconstrained formulation via design is possible	**Poor policy design space** Only partially informed or restricted design is possible
	Less instrumental	**Capable political non-design space** Relatively unconstrained non-design processes are possible	**Poor political non-design space** Only poorly informed non-design is possible

Source: Chindarkar et al. (2017).

can ensue from incomplete knowledge and information or less technical and more overtly political forms of policy-making ("non-designs")
which embody less evidence problem solution-related information and
knowledge are likely to occur.

Table 1.3 presents a schematic illustration of how these two different
aspects of policy-making – a design intention and the capacity to carry
it out – create different policy formulation spaces which enable very
different policy processes.

How do designs change?

Several common ways in which designs emerge have been identified
in the policy studies literature. Examples of brand new policy designs
are, of course, very few. Most policy initiatives rather deal with already
created policies with significant historical legacies, and can be hampered
due to reforms and revisions at various points in their history which
have attempted to address and correct problems which have emerged
as the policy has evolved over time. In this case, the introduction of
new elements may conflict with pre-existing policy components and
cause further difficulties (Carey et al. 2017). Although other policy instrument groupings could theoretically be more successful in achieving
policy goals, it may be very difficult to accomplish or even propose
wholesale changes, and designs instead often focus on reform rather than
replacement of an existing arrangement. 'lock in' often leads to *layering*
in which processes of (re)design alter only some aspects of a pre-existing
arrangement, adding new elements to an existing policy often without

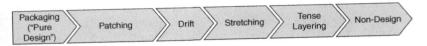

Figure 1.1 A spectrum of design processes.
Source: Howlett and Mukherjee (2014).

abandoning previous ones. This can easily lead to internal contradictions emerging between tools and goals within policy mixes, and mixes of policy elements can emerge over long stretches of time as a result of successive policy decisions which are not necessarily logically integrated.

Students of policy formulation and policy design are thus very interested in how policy formulators, like software designers, rather than replace existing packages, instead often issue more modest 'patches' in order to correct flaws in existing mixes or allow them to adapt to changing circumstances (Howlett and Rayner 2013). Poor patching can involve policy *stretching* (Feindt and Flynn 2009) where, sometimes operating over periods of decades or more, elements of a mix are simply extended to cover areas they were not intended to at the outset. Such 'stretching' is problematic as small changes in policy environments can create a situation where the elements of a mix can fail to be mutually supportive, frustrating initial policy goals.

As Figure 1.1 shows, forms of policy formulation move from highly intentional and instrumental design efforts to those which are more partial and less intentional, such as 'smart' patching, and ultimately to those which involve poor design such as 'stretching' and poor, or "tense", layering. In cases such as these, formulation introduces progressively more severe inconsistencies and incongruencies and tensions between policy layers and policy-making, exacerbating the challenges faced by policy designers. These and other topics are taken up in the following chapters.

References

Bobrow, Davis. "Policy Design: Ubiquitous, Necessary and Difficult." In *Handbook of Public Policy*, edited by Guy Peters, B. and Jon Pierre, 75–96. Beverly Hills, CA: SAGE, 2006.

Carey, Gemma, Adrian Kay, and Ann Nevile. "Institutional Legacies and 'Sticky Layers': What Happens in Cases of Transformative Policy Change?" *Administration & Society* 51, no. 3 (2019): 491–509. doi:10.1177/0095399717704682.

Chindarkar, Namrata, Michael Howlett, and M. Ramesh. "Conceptualizing Effective Social Policy Design: Design Spaces and Capacity Challenges." *Public Administration and Development* 37, no. 1 (February 1, 2017): 3–14.

May, Peter J. "Policy Design and Implementation." In Handbook of Public Administration, edited by Guy Peters, B. and Jon Pierre, 223–33. Beverly Hills, CA: Sage, 2003.

Feindt, Peter H., and Andrew Flynn. "Policy Stretching and Institutional Layering: British Food Policy between Security, Safety, Quality, Health and Climate Change." *British Politics* 4, no. 3 (2009): 386–414.

Goldsmith, S., and W. D. Eggers. *Governing by Network: The New Shape of the Public Sector.* Washington D.C.: Brookings Institution Press, 2004.

Goodin, Robert E. *Manipulatory Politics.* New Haven, CT: Yale University Press, 1980.

Hood, Christopher. *The Tools of Government.* Chatham: Chatham House Publishers, 1986.

Howlett, Michael. "Governance Modes, Policy Regimes and Operational Plans: A Multi-Level Nested Model of Policy Instrument Choice and Policy Design." *Policy Sciences* 42, no. 1 (2009): 73–89.

Howlett, Michael. *Designing Public Policies: Principles and Instruments.* New York: Routledge, 2011.

Howlett, Michael, and Ishani Mukherjee. "Policy Design and Non-Design: Towards a Spectrum of Policy Formulation Types." *Politics and Governance* 2, no. 2 (November 13, 2014): 57–71.

Howlett, Michael, M. Ramesh, and Anthony Perl. *Studying Public Policy: Policy Cycles & Policy Subsystems.* Toronto: Oxford University Press, 2009.

Howlett, Michael, and Jeremy Rayner. "Patching vs Packaging in Policy Formulation: Assessing Policy Portfolio Design." *Politics and Governance* 1, no. 2 (2013): 170–82.

Klijn, Erik-Hans, Joop Koppenjan, and Katrien Termeer. "Managing Networks in the Public Sector: A Theoretical Study of Management Strategies in Policy Networks." *Public Administration* 73 (1995): 437–54.

Lasswell, Harold D. "The Policy Orientation." In *The Policy Sciences: Recent Developments in Scope and Method,* edited by Daniel Lerner and Harold D. Lasswell, 3–15. Stanford, CA: Stanford University Press, 1951.

Linder, Stephen H., and B. Guy Peters. "From Social Theory to Policy Design." *Journal of Public Policy* 4, no. 3 (1984): 237–59.

Linder, Steven H., and B. Guy Peters. "The Logic of Public Policy Design: Linking Policy Actors and Plausible Instruments." *Knowledge in Society* 4 (1991): 125–51.

Salamon, Lester M. "Rethinking Public Management: Third-Party Government and the Changing Forms of Government Action." *Public Policy* 29, no. 3 (1981): 255–75.

Salamon, Lester M. *The Tools of Government: A Guide to the New Governance.* New York: Oxford University Press, 2002.Vedung, Evert. "Policy Instruments: Typologies and Theories." In *Carrots, Sticks and Sermons: Policy Instruments and Their Evaluation,* edited by Marie-Louise Bemelmans-Videc, Ray C. Rist, and Evert Oskar Vedung, 21–58. New Brunswick, NJ: Transaction Publishers, 1997.

Wildavsky, Aaron B. *Speaking Truth to Power: The Art and Craft of Policy Analysis.* Boston, MA: Little-Brown, 1979.

2 Systematically studying policy design

The logic of tool use

Policy design is a specific form of policy formulation based on the gathering and application of knowledge about policy tools to the development and implementation of programmes aimed at the attainment of desired policy ambitions. In a time when policy-makers are often tasked with developing large-scale innovative solutions to increasingly complex policy problems, such as climate or demographic change, the need for intelligent design of policies and a better understanding of the policy formulation processes they involve has never been greater.

In general, as we have seen, a means–ends understanding of policy formulation permeates the policy design orientation (Colebatch 2018). Although, as Chapter 1 noted, policy-making does not always necessarily lend itself to, or result in, purely instrumental thinking about policy issues, this instrumental orientation is significant in that policy formulators operating in accordance with its strictures are expected to base their actions on analyses which are logical and knowledge- and evidence-based (Bhatta 2002).

In this sense, the design of a policy, conceptually at least, can be divorced from the vagaries of formulation and imaginary constructs and schemes can be created by organizations such as think tanks and public policy research institutes who develop and propose not necessarily immediately realizable designs. These include, for example, proposals made in the recent past, proposals for carbon taxes, healthcare accounts and educational voucher systems. This is not an unusual a practice in the design world, and is much the same phenomenon which occurs daily with respect to, for example, building designs where an architect develops an ideal or abstract design which is fully expected to be altered to meet the needs and demands of clients, and in order to conform with engineering principles, weather and soil conditions and local building codes, among other constraints (Ingraham 1987).

Conceptually, such instrumentally oriented policy design processes, like building designs and others, begins with an assessment of the materials available for construction, in this case the abilities of different policy tools or levers to affect policy outputs and outcomes, followed by considerations of the availability of the resources or materials required to allow a policy to operate as intended and the demand or desire for them to be used. As Linder and Peters (1991) noted, this involves a series of analyses which emphasize 'not only the potential for generating new mixtures of conventional solutions, but also the importance of giving careful attention to tradeoffs among design criteria when considering instrument choices' (130). Designing policies in this way is not simple. It requires an understanding of how the use of specific kinds of instruments affects target group behaviour and compliance with government aims (Weaver 2015), and knowledge and consideration of the many constraints on tool use originating in the limits of existing knowledge and prevailing government priorities and governance structures (Torgerson 1986). It also requires both analytical and evidentiary capacity on the part of the government as well as the intention to exercise it (Howlett 2015). Nevertheless within policy studies the payoff from such activities is expected to be large and well worth the effort on all but the simplest occasions.

Knowledge limitations affecting policy design

One constraint which policy designers face involves limitations on the kinds of knowledge target of behaviour and future states of affairs which they can compile without undue hardship. In 1957, Herbert Simon developed the concept of 'bounded rationality' to characterize the world in which decision-makers operate, highlighting the gap existing between actual human choice processes and administrative theory which often ignored cognitive and other knowledge limits on proposals for policy and programme designs (Simon 1957). According to this view, human beings never have full knowledge of the future nor the time and resources which would allow them to consider all possible courses of action and arrive a maximizing decisions. Instead, for Simon, they operate within the bounds of the limits on their cognition in undertaking any activity, including policy-making, meaning even the best designs can be thought of as merely 'satisfactory' rather than optimal in nature.

This is not to say that policies are irrational and that the effort to apply logic and evidence to policy-making activities is fruitless, but rather to highlight the extent to which activities like policy design are influenced by the pre-conceptions and heuristics which policy-makers bring to their tasks. It also serves as a precautionary warning to erstwhile designers of the high likelihood their designs will not work perfectly as intended but will encounter some unexpected circumstances and impacts which, like extreme weather events in engineering, must also be incorporated into designs to ensure their resilience and robustness in the face of adverse circumstances.

Within this framework of knowledge limitations, what is it that policy designers and designs seek to accomplish? Here, it is reasonable to suggest that all policies are geared towards deploying state resources towards altering the behaviour of some policy 'target' and that they usually seek to do so in a *persuasive* way (Redström 2006), that is, in a way that secures maximum compliance of the targets with government aims with minimal government effort.

Compliance is itself a complex subject, however, embodies a great deal of uncertainty with respect to human behaviour and what kinds of policy interventions affect it and in what ways (May 2004). Determining exactly why certain actors comply with government actions while others do not or less so is a key aspect of contemporary design research and is discussed in further detail below.

While it is often assumed that such government policy efforts can be effortlessly or 'seamlessly calibrated' to solve the fundamental issue at stake with exactly the appropriate amount of effort and resources, like knowledge limitation issues, compliance unknowns also result in a high level of uncertainty that affects both policy designs and designers (Manski 2011). Empirical evidence, not surprisingly, suggests a complex pattern of target responses to policy actions is common in which few efforts are well calibrated to the problem at hand, while many either systematically under- or overreact to a problem, often oscillating between these two states (Maor 2017). As Table 2.1 shows, in two of four possible cases, well-calibrated designs may occur, but there is always the possibility of two other cases when *disproportionate* policy reactions over- or under'shoot' the severity of the problem and do not adequately match the nature of the underlying problem. What's more, such over and under-reactions can be deliberate or accidental, meaning they may sometimes be planned and part of design considerations and at other times not.

As Simon (1973) also pointed out many years ago, a third aspect of uncertainty relates to the fact that social problems come in different shapes and forms, and the extent of available knowledge and the ability and desire of decision-makers to incorporate that knowledge into their thinking varies across issue areas.

Table 2.1 Cases of disproportional policy reaction and design

	Nature of policy design problem	
Nature of policy response	*Simple*	*Large/Complex*
Simple	Proportionate design (e.g. Automobile speeding)	Under-design (e.g. Climate change)
Large/Complex	Over-design (e.g. National security)	Proportionate design (e.g. Air traffic regulation)

That is, some problems are 'well-structured' in the sense that their causes and effects, and the means to deal with them, are relatively well known, while others are ill-structured in the sense that knowledge of problems and solutions is unknown or unrealized and the level of uncertainty with which they can be grappled is much higher. This is the basis for the distinction made in the 1970s by Rittel and Weber (1973) between 'wicked' and 'tame' problems (see Table 2.2) which also is a concern for policy design.

Table 2.2 Tame and wicked problems

		Nature of knowledge of the problem	
		Known/Well-defined and understood	*Unknown/Ill-defined*
Nature of knowledge of the solution	*Known/well-defined and understood*	Well-Structured ('Tame problem') e.g. Automobile traffic control/street racing	Ill-Structured Problem e.g. Tobacco control/ addiction
	Unknown/ Ill-defined	Ill-Structured solution e.g. Homelessness	Poorly structured ("Wicked Problem") e.g. Climate Change

Even more complex design challenges exist when both the level of 'objective' knowledge of problems and the relative nature of decision-makers' knowledge of that 'fact-base' are taken into account; or if there is little agreement on the choice of variables to be included in models (Chow and Sarin 2002) (see Table 2.3).

Table 2.3 Policy-maker's knowledge and comprehension matrix

		Nature of existing knowledge of a phenomenon	
		Aspects of the problem and possible solutions are known	*Aspects are unknown*
Nature of decision-makers' awareness of existing knowledge of a phenomenon	*Aware*	Known-known: Key policy actors are aware of the known aspects of a phenomena (INFORMED AWARENESS)	Known-unknown: Key policy actors are aware that certain aspects of the phenomenon are unknow‌ (PRUDENT AWARENES‌
	Ignorant	Unknown-Known: Key policy actors are unaware of known aspects of a phenomenon (UNINFORMED IGNORANCE)	Unknown-Unknown: Key policy actors are unawa‌ that certain aspects of the phenomenon are unknow‌ (IMPRUDENT IGNORANCE)

Behavioural considerations

Notwithstanding these epistemological challenges, the aim of most public policy remains to invoke desired behavioural change in the 'targets' of government efforts through deployment of governing resources in the form of substantive and procedural policy tools aimed at that behaviour.

This process of behavioural change involves at least four linkages, all of which are affected by contextual aspects present at the moment at which instruments are invoked and behavioural mechanisms triggered. These are: (1) the link between tools and the governing resources present at any moment in time, (2) the link between these resources and the mechanisms which tools activate, (3) the link between the mechanisms and the actual behavioural changes which occur post-activation and (4) the link between changes in behaviour and policy outputs.

All four of these linkages are susceptible to various barriers and impediments to instrument choices, mechanism activation, reception and impact, which make policy design and designing complex and error-prone activities. There are many such barriers and intermediating factors, which include such factors as a preferred policy style and governance mode which can affect preferences for certain tools over others; the various capacity strengths and weaknesses which can limit the capability of governments to use particular tools or eliminate their use altogether; possible countervailing demands and constraints on behavioural change which can undermine the effect and impact of a mechanisms; as well as various kinds of implementation and other issues which can lessen, or enhance, policy outputs (see Figure 2.1).

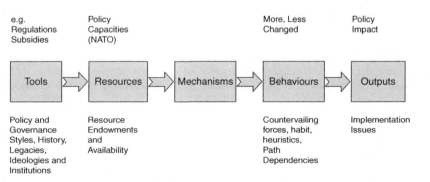

Contextual Barriers and Constraints

Figure 2.1 Context-related mechanism constraints.

In general, two kinds of design-relevant policy mechanisms can be identified: those which more or less directly affect actor behaviour and those which involve learning and more reflective activities. Although often assumed or regarded purely at the level of individuals, many of these mechanisms also operate at the more collective or group level.

In this view, at the individual level, the mechanisms activated by policy instruments in order to trigger policy change are characteristics of human behaviour such as greed, fear, risk aversion, or the use of heuristics and others which affect the logics of calculation and appropriateness individuals take towards such issues as whether or not to perform a crime, quit smoking, invest in a pension fund or donate to a charity (see Figure 2.2).

These kinds of mechanisms are triggered or activated by 'substantive' policy instruments, and one of the main reasons one tool would be chosen over another is often supply-oriented: that is, a government will utilize specific kinds of tools deploying the resources it has in ample supply or which can be easily replenished (Hood 1983). This is an important insight. But in addition to 'supply-side' capacity issues, as discussed above, 'demand-side' considerations are also very significant in policy design. That is, in general, each category of policy tool involves the use of a specific governing resource expected to trigger or lever a specific characteristic or receptor in a target, inducing a certain behavioural response. Thus, the effectiveness of the deployment of such tools is linked not just to resource availability – a precondition of their use – but also to the existence of different 'receptors' on the part of policy targets which make them respond in a predictable way to the use of this resource.

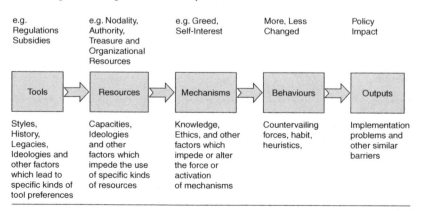

Figure 2.2 Links in the design chain – individual and group levels.

Resources are used and tools deployed in order to secure better compliance or adherence of populations to government aims and ambitions, be it in the promotion of public safety and security or in the provision of effective healthcare and social welfare. If perfect compliance with governments' aims existed automatically, of course, there would be little need to undertake state activity beyond information provision in that a government would only have to inform citizens of its ambitions for perfect compliance to occur. But, of course, it does not. Desired changes can be large or small, and the expectation of compliance can be rapid or gradual, but in all cases, some changes in behaviour in a direction congruent with government aims are expected to require the utilization of other kinds of state resources.

Traditionally, much compliance theory in economics and elsewhere has been based on a fairly superficial concept of target behaviour involving 'deterrence' (Kaine et al. 2010) in which the primary type of tool to be deployed to acheive a policy goal is a penalty. This is based upon the hedonic idea that narrow self-interest and calculable utility in enhancing pleasure and avoiding pain are the primary motivators of compliance behaviour on the part of policy actors, with governments enhancing pain through penalties (and often pleasure through subsidies) in efforts to deter or encourage specific kinds of activity.

In practice, this means that compliance of policy targets with government intentions is often viewed as a problem equated with the exercise of authority on the part of governments in the form of laws and regulations designed to deter certain kinds of activity, sometimes coupled with other kinds of incentives – often financial – that encourage other kinds. Compliance-deterrence utility considerations can then be extended to the calculation of the more precise calibration of such tools, with incentives and disincentives set at such a level as to punish those who might contest the legitimacy of such actions or seek to free-ride on compliers and/or reward those who comply.

As suggested earlier, however, the situation is more complex than a purely utilitarian perspective would have it, as even the most basic activities of governance such as paying taxes and obeying rules involve not just individual hedonic behaviour but also considerations on the part of targets and the public concerning the legality and normative 'appropriateness' of government's levying and collecting such taxes (March and Olsen 1989). Moreover, different kinds of target groups and individuals exist (and are perceived to exist) and can be and are treated differently by governments in terms of government expectations of the nature of their compliant or non-compliant behaviour (Schneider and Ingram 1994).

Some targets, for example, such as businesses may be thought to be influenced through means such as financial incentives or penalities while others, such as parents, may be thought to respond better to efforts at moral suasion and education. But the compliance situation is made even more complex by the fact that different targets have different resources and capabilities and attitudes when it comes to determining whether or not they will comply, and how, and to what extent, they will not. These attitudes can be quite complex and rooted in historical and culturally specific views of government intentions and the moral and other aspects of compliant and non-compliant behaviour (Wan et al. 2015). These can include, for example, considerations of the legitimacy and illegitimacy of government actors and actions in specific fields such as constitutional, religious or privacy-related ones, but can also run into and involve desires on the part of individuals and groups to earn praise, or avoid shame, or to avoid guilt and social opprobrium for their actions.

This variation in target motivation and compliance behaviour makes policy design a much more challenging activity than that surmised from either a bounded-rationality perspective on policy knowledge or a simple hedonic utilitarian perspective. Whether a proposed action triggers behaviour linked to 'affiliation' or 'conformity' with government wishes or results in 'boomerang' effects (encouraging the action it is aimed at discouraging, or vice versa, such as sometimes happens from, for example, the increased prominence or normalizing of smoking or unsafe sexual activity featured in government anti-smoking and public health campaigns) is critical but not well understood. And neither is the effect of the manner in which compliance can be affected by the type of 'message' sent, urging compliance and its negative or positive nature, the way it has been framed, as well as other factors linked to the character of the underlying norm itself (see also Schultz et al. 2007). What works with one individual or group may not work with another, and it is not unusual for a range of governing resources and tools to have to be deployed in order to deal with such complex, 'target-rich' environments.

In such circumstances, governments must determine not only whether or not a target is likely to comply with government actions and intentions but also whether or the extent to which compliance will be reluctantly or freely given. As Table 2.4 shows, estimations and diagnoses about likely compliance behaviour can usefully be linked to coercive versus persuasive actions on the part of governments.

Table 2.4 Nature of compliance of policy targets

		Likelihood of compliance	
		High	Low
Willingness to comply	High	Model subjects Requires little coercion, education or persuasion	Reluctant subjects Requires education and persuasion
	Low	Resistant subjects Requires incentives to comply	Combative subjects Requires a high level of coercion and monitoring to compel compliance

Source: Modelled after Scholz (1991).

How governments perceive targets and classify groups within them is another critical aspect of policy design, but as Schneider and Ingram (1993 and 1994) have repeatedly pointed out, there are some limits to the ability of governments to discern the true nature of these relationships. The expected behaviour of policy targets is often framed by government agencies using the dual aspects of 'positive' or 'negative' stereotypes and whether they are powerful or weak actors in society. These social constructions of target populations are often created by politics, culture, socialization, history, media, literature, religion and the like. Positive constructions include images such as 'deserving', 'intelligent', 'honest', 'public spirited'. Negative constructions include images such as 'undeserving', 'stupid', 'dishonest' and 'selfish' (See Table 2.5). Both constructions may be inaccurate but can lead to the use of specific kinds of tools regardless of their actual impact.

Table 2.5 Perceptions of policy targets after Schneider and Ingram (1993)

		Conception of social role	
		Positive	Negative
Conception of power	Strong/powerful	Advantaged Subsidies and incentives	Adversaries Regulation and controls
	Weak/vulnerable	Dependents Moral suasion and exhortation	Deviants Coercion and punishments, disincentives

Source: Modelled after Schneider and Ingram (1993).

In practice, therefore, the types of tools used to address problems involving these groups often vary directly according to their categorization, with positively viewed targets receiving benefits and negatively viewed ones 'burdened' by costs. More coercive measures are often used against groups perceived as 'deviants' rather than against other groups who might actually be more resistant to government initiatives, while tools such as subsidies and other kinds of payments might be most effective if used in dealing with 'dependents' but are often given instead to advantaged groups.

This discussion highlights the significant linkages which exist between both perceptions of and actual target behaviour and government tool use. Accurately determining this requires research and clarity on the part of government and the avoidance of stereotypes and simple estimations of target group attitudes and power. Of course, while there is no denying that targets are politically and socially constructed, there is also a significant 'objective' linkage in expectations governments have about compliance. That is, advantaged groups are usually expected to comply or have similar interests or share government aspirations in general more than do deviants, and dependents are often able to evade controls in the same way as do adversary groups (Pierce et al. 2014).

Improving policy designs through better linking tools, mechanisms and targets

The fundamental design problem for governments then, is not just determining a given governmental resource endowment or calculating the range of prison sentences or the amount of fines and subsidies to levy in some situation based on a utilitarian compliance-deterrence logic, but rather to understand on which basis compliance is likely to occur or not.

This is a design challenge which requires detailed empirical investigation and analysis in each case of tool deployment, and continued monitoring over time to ensure these fundamental conditions have not changed or been undermined by any action undertaken. Governments enjoying a high level of trust, for example, may be able to undertake actions through moral suasion, while those which do not enjoy that credibility will need to employ other tools. But whether or not this high level of trust is being maintained is a key determinant of policy effectiveness, and continual monitoring and assessment is required to ensure this remains the case and that existing tools continue to function effectively over time.

Table 2.6 presents some of the behavioural prerequisites which governing tools rely upon for their effects.

Table 2.6 Behavioural needs for resource effectiveness

Tool type	Resource applied	Target behavioural pre-requisite
Nodality	Information	Credibility/trust – willingness to believe and act on information provided by government
Authority	Coercive power/force	Legitimacy – willingness to be manipulated by government invoked penalties and proscriptions
Treasure	Financial	Cupidity – willingness to be manipulated by gain/losses imposed by governments
Organization	Organization	Competence – willingness to receive goods and services from government and enter into partnership arrangements

Source: Howlett (2011).

In the case of information use, for example, tool effectiveness relies both on the availability of knowledge and the means to distribute it ('resources') and on the target's belief in the accuracy of the messages being purveyed, or their *credibility* ('receptor'). Similarly, the effectiveness of the use of authoritative tools, as discussed earlier, depends not just on the availability of coercive mechanisms and their enforcement, but also on target perceptions of government *legitimacy*. Similarly, the effective use of treasure resources depends not just on the availability of government funding, but also on target groups' financial need and especially their receptivity to government funding or their *cupidity*. Likewise, the effective use of organizational tools depends both on the existence of personnel and other organizational resource and on target group perceptions of government *competence* and fairness in the deployment and training of personnel to provide services and rules (Howlett 2017).

These are important considerations in policy design and especially in the calibration of policy tools. Thus, the use of authority-based tools such as laws and regulations, for example, involves considerations of legitimacy on the part of targets but must not overreach or overburden the extent of legitimacy which a government enjoys. If a policy measure does so, it most assuredly will require much monitoring and enforcement activity in order to be even minimally effective, involving large administrative costs and burdens which may well undermine its own efficiency and effectiveness, as has occurred in the past in many countries in areas such as cannabis or alcohol prohibition.

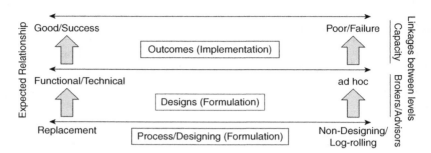

Figure 2.3 Policy effectiveness as the relationship between process, design and outcome.

In general, contemporary design scholars argue that feasible and realizable alternatives will be generated through design oriented policy formulation processes and that such alternatives will emerge triumphant in deliberations and conflicts involved in decisions to adopt certain tools and not others. In other words, policy effectiveness is a multi-level phenomenon in which process, design and outcome are linked closely together (see Figure 2.3).

That is, the overall supposition of design studies in this field is one in which there is an expectation that a superior process of policy formulation ('designing') will lead to a superior set of policy instruments and components ('design') which will, in turn, result in a superior outcome than would be accomplished using some other kind of process – such as pure bargaining or log-rolling. However, as was pointed out in Chapter 1, there is no necessary link or guarantee that this will occur. The kinds of knowledge and behaviour limits cited above generate many uncertainties about the effectiveness of designs and measures taken to implement them which are unavoidable and must be taken into account in translating abstract designs into achievable on-the-ground ones. Different tools have different capabilities in this regard and knowledge of the strengths and weaknesses of the basic building blocks of policy action in areas such as compliance and targeting is essential to anyone attempting to fashion, or study, policy designing.

Conclusion: policy design as instrumental knowledge mobilization

The modern policy studies movement began with the recognition that public policy-making results from the interactions of policy-makers in the exercise of power, legitimate or otherwise. Although some of these policy-making efforts may be arbitrary or capricious, most can be viewed as representing the concerted and intentional efforts of actors attempting to have governments act instrumentally in a process of policy design; that is, to achieve a particular policy goal or end through the use and deployment of a set of relatively well-known set of policy means developed over many years of state-building and experience.

Of course, these goals can be wide-ranging and often pose no small amount of difficulty and complexity in both their definition and diagnosis. This means the formulation of solutions that are likely to succeed in addressing them necessitates the systematic consideration of the impact and feasibility of the use of specific kinds of policy means or instruments and the conditions of supply and demand around them.

Early work often depicted policy design as a specific kind of policy-making in which knowledge of the policy impacts of specific policy tools was combined with the practical capacity of governments to identify and implement the most suitable technical means in the effort to achieve a specific policy aim. This activity was expected to occur *ex ante* and independently of other considerations, such as political or personal gain, which might also affect formulation processes and activities.

Later works examining instances of actual 'design' activity recognized it as requiring a situation where there was both support for policy analysis and design work on the part of policy-makers and also a low policy 'lock-in' on existing policy and programme arrangements which made more sweeping designs possible. Such favourable design circumstances were seen to be rare and closely coupled with the presence of a high level of capacity and expertise on the part of policy analysts and decision-makers which could mobilize knowledge effectively so that policy instruments were effectively and efficiently matched to policy goals and targets.

In the present era, it is argued that when all such conditions are present, purposive design activity is possible and preferable to other forms of policy formulation, and that such circumstances can at least be partially engineered through the promotion of knowledge-based advice and in policy-making. This can be seen for example, recent efforts at enhancing knowledge mobilization through the promotion of 'evidence-based policy-making' or the effort to enhance, develop and mobilize the use of knowledge in policy-making efforts, notably in health but extending to many other policy domains as well. When these conditions are not, however, less technical and more overtly political forms of policy-making, the propensity for over- and under-design and less effective or ineffective policy outcomes are thought to be more likely to ensue.

The fervent wish of proponents of the design orientation both then and now, however, has been to reduce the latter instances to as few as possible by promoting the kinds of orientations and dedication of resources required for better-designed policies to emerge, those thought to be more likely to solve pressing problems, correct social ills and serve the public good (Azuela and Barroso 2012).

How this can be done on the ground and what are the characteristics of the various types of tools which go into the make-up of policies are the subjects of the four chapters found in the next section of the book.

References

Azuela, Gabriela Elizondo, and Luiz Augusto Barroso. *Design and Performance of Policy Instruments to Promote the Development of Renewable Energy: Emerging Experience in Selected Developing Countries.* Washington, DC: World Bank Publications, 2012.

Bhatta, Gambhir. "Evidence-Based Analysis and the Work of Policy Shops." *Australian Journal of Public Administration* 61, no. 3 (2002): 98–105.

Chow, Clare Chua, and Rakesh K. Sarin. "Known, Unknown, and Unknowable Uncertainties." *Theory and Decision* 52, no. 2 (March 1, 2002): 127–38.

Colebatch, H. K. "The Idea of Policy Design: Intention, Process, Outcome, Meaning and Validity." *Public Policy and Administration* 33, no. 4 (October 1, 2018): 365–83.

Hood, C. "Using Bureaucracy Sparingly." *Public Administration* 61, no. 2 (1983): 197–208.

Howlett, Michael. "Policy Analytical Capacity: The Supply and Demand for Policy Analysis in Government." *Policy and Society*, Special Issue on the Dynamics of Policy Capacity, 34, no. 3 (September 1, 2015): 173–82.

Howlett, Michael. "Matching Policy Tools and Their Targets: Beyond Nudges and Utility Maximisation in Policy Design." *Policy & Politics*, 46, no. 1 (January 18, 2018): 101–24.

Ingraham, Patricia W. "Towards More Systemic Consideration of Policy Design." *Policy Studies Journal* 15, no. 4 (1987): 611–28.

Kaine, Geoff, Helen Murdoch, Ruth Lourey, and Denise Bewsell. "A Framework for Understanding Individual Response to Regulation." *Food Policy* 35, no. 6 (December 2010): 531–37.

Linder, S. H., and B. G. Peters. "The Logic of Public Policy Design: Linking Policy Actors and Plausible Instruments." *Knowledge in Society* 4 (1991): 125–51.

Manski, Charles F. "Policy Analysis with Incredible Certitude." *The Economic Journal* 121, no. 554 (August 1, 2011): F261–89.

Maor, Moshe. "The Implications of the Emerging Disproportionate Policy Perspective for the New Policy Design Studies." *Policy Sciences* 50, no. 3 (September 1, 2017): 383–98.

March, J. G., and J. P. Olsen. *Rediscovering Institutions: The Organizational Basis of Politics.* New York: The Free Press, 1989.

May, Peter J. "Compliance Motivations: Affirmative and Negative Bases." *Law & Society Review* 38, no. 1 (2004): 41–68.

Pierce, Jonathan J., Saba Siddiki, Michael D. Jones, Kristin Schumacher, Andrew Pattison, and Holly Peterson. "Social Construction and Policy Design: A Review of Past Applications." *Policy Studies Journal* 42, no. 1 (February 1, 2014): 1–29.

Redström, Johan. "Persuasive Design: Fringes and Foundations." In *Persuasive Technology,* edited by Wijnand A. IJsselsteijn, Yvonne A. W. de Kort, Cees Midden, Berry Eggen, and Elise van den Hoven, 112–22. Lecture Notes in Computer Science 3962. Berlin and Heidelberg: Springer, 2006.

Rittel, H. W. J., and M. M. Webber. "Dilemmas in a General Theory of Planning." *Policy Sciences* 4 (1973): 155–69.

Schneider, A., and H. Ingram. "Social Construction of Target Populations: Implications for Politics and Policy." *American Political Science Review* 87, no. 2 (1993): 334–47.

Schneider, A., and H. Ingram. "Social Constructions and Policy Design: Implications for Public Administration." *Research in Public Administration* 3 (1994): 137–73.

Scholz, J. T. "Cooperative Regulatory Enforcement and the Politics of Administrative Effectiveness." *American Political Science Review* 85, no. 1 (1991): 115–36.

Schultz, P. Wesley, Jessica M. Nolan, Robert B. Cialdini, Noah J. Goldstein, and Vladas Griskevicius. "The Constructive, Destructive, and Reconstructive Power of Social Norms." *Psychological Science* 18, no. 5 (May 1, 2007): 429–34.

Simon, Herbert A. *Models of Man, Social and Rational: Mathematical Essays on Rational Human Behavior in a Social Setting.* New York: Wiley, 1957.

Simon, Herbert A. "The Structure of Ill Structured Problems." *Artificial Intelligence* 4, no. 3–4 (Winter 1973): 181–201.

Torgerson, D. "Between Knowledge and Politics: Three Faces Of Policy Analysis." *Policy Sciences* 19, no. 1 (1986): 33–59.

Wan, Calvin, Geoffrey Qiping Shen, and Ann Yu. "Key Determinants of Willingness to Support Policy Measures on Recycling: A Case Study in Hong Kong." *Environmental Science & Policy* 54 (December 2015): 409–18.

Weaver, R. Kent. "Getting People to Behave: Research Lessons for Policy Makers." *Public Administration Review* 75, no. 6 (2015): 806–16.

Part II

Policy tools – the building blocks of policy designs

3 Organizational implementation tools

Organizational implementation instruments are a class of policy tools that is amongst the oldest and most often utilized, a common feature of government and governance in all countries and jurisdictions. This category of tools includes a broad range of governing instruments which *rely upon the use of government and non-governmental institutions and personnel to affect policy output delivery and policy process change.*

There is a wide variety of *substantive organizational tools* available to governments wishing to affect both the production and the consumption/distribution of goods and services in society. These generally fall into two main types, depending on the proximity of their relationship to government and hence the ability of government to control the effects of their utilization. Subtypes include direct government and quasi-governmental or societally based organizational tools. *Procedural organizational tools* generally involve the organization and reorganization of government agencies and policy processes in order to affect key parameters of governmental activity and that of the actors arrayed in policy communities and networks which governments face in making public policies.

Substantive organizational instruments

There are many types of substantive instruments which fall into this category. Most involve (and rely primarily) on the use of government personnel to achieve government goals, usually operating in structures created and controlled by governments. 'Direct' government organizations or classical administrative agencies of various kinds and names form the backbone of this category, but it also includes 'indirect' or quasi- or parastatal ones. One of the best-known examples of the latter is the state-owned or 'public enterprise' – which itself comes in many shapes, sizes, colours and flavours (Bernier 2011). But other non-state-based ones also exist such as co-production or certification tools which also engage or supplant government personnel in their implementation (Cashore 2004; Voorberg et al. 2015).

Most policy mixes contain at least one organizational tool, often at the centre of a web or mix of other tools which serve to supplement that instrument, extend its range or control for spill-overs and other problems associated with pure government administration. This is the case, for example, which a health department which serves at the centre of a network of other kinds of organizations like hospitals, clinics, pharmaceutical companies and the like engaged in health service delivery. The general nature of each of these major types of organizational tools and the reasons for their use are described below.

Direct government

The direct use of government agencies for substantive policy purposes involves the 'delivery of a good or service by government employees, funded by appropriations from government treasury' (Leman 1989; Leman and Salamon 2002). This is what is sometimes referred to as 'the forgotten fundamental' within policy instrument studies, as its ubiquitous nature is often ignored in studies which take it for granted and focus instead on more esoteric kinds of tools.

Within this general type of direct government organizational tool, there are several common forms or subtypes found in many jurisdictions. These include the following.

Line departments

In most countries, government agencies undertake a very wide variety of tasks on a direct basis. These services are provided at all levels of government (central or federal, provincial, state or regional, as well as urban or local) in slightly different configurations in different countries but often through core departments or what are sometimes referred to as 'line' departments in order to distinguish them from 'staff' agencies which typically co-ordinate rather than deliver services themselves. Unemployment, welfare or social security payments, for example, can be the task of central governments in some countries and eras, and of provincial or local governments in others but are commonly administered by line departments or their functional equivalents.

Typically, these kinds of government agencies follow what is known in the public administration literature as a Weberian 'monocratic bureaucracy' form of organization (Rudolph and Rudolph 1979). This is a type of organizational structure first systematically described and analyzed by the German political sociologist Max Weber (1978) in his early twentieth-century work, *Economy and Society*. Weber argued that although bureaucratic forms of organization had a long history in ancient and medieval empires and kingdoms, a significant change had occurred in the modern era – roughly corresponding to the start of the French Revolution in the late eighteenth century – when such organizations came to be viewed as providing services to the public rather than being the property of a monarch or emperor to do with as he or she pleased (Albrow 1970). The main characteristics of these modern government agencies, in Weber's view, were:

- Personnel are appointed on the basis of a merit system of appointment, retention and recruitment.
- Office holders do not own the office in which they work, but hold it subject to the provisions of the merit system.
- Offices tend to be organized in a hierarchical fashion, with a relatively small span of control, and multiple levels.
- All activities in the agency operate according to the rule of law – that office holders are not above the law and must operate within its limits (including provisions for their accountability – via some form of 'chain of accountability' – to representative assemblies in modern liberal democracies who actually establish and promulgate laws).

(Weber 1978)

Line departments have this 'classic' hierarchical Weberian monocratic bureaucratic form and are thoroughly embedded in the legal forms of governance associated with them. Such units are typically organized in a pyramidal shape, linking offices of civil servants in various branches and sections to a single department head, such as a department of health or a department of highways. Sub-variations of this include the 'ministry', a form in which typically multiple pyramids of departments culminate in a single head (e.g. a ministry of lands, parks and housing), or an 'agency' which operates semi-autonomously from the policy-making level (itself often termed a 'ministry') (Verhoest et al. 2012).

Regardless of the specifics, these forms of government organization are the 'workhorses' providing most publicly provided goods and services in most modern states (see Table 3.1 for an example of their use in government service delivery in one such modern state, Canada).

In most countries, the size and number of government agencies have grown dramatically over the past two centuries through the creation

Table 3.1 Tasks typically undertaken by government agencies

Task	Examples
Facilitating commerce	Mint, standards of weights and measures bureaus
Managing public lands	Commissioners of public lands, ministries of lands and parks or environment or natural resources
Constructing public works	Departments of public works – airports, highways
Research, testing and statistics	National statistical agencies
Law and justice	Courts, solicitor-general or attorney general offices, corrections and prisons, policing
Technical assistance, record-keeping and libraries	Farm extension, ministries of agriculture, national archives, national libraries
Healthcare	Ministries of health – hospitals. clinics, dentists, nursing, home care.
Social services	Ministries of welfare and social, family or community services
Education and training	Ministries of education, post-secondary education colleges and universities, technical and training institutes
Labour relations	Ministries of labour and labour relations.
Marketing	Tourism, ministries of small business, ministries of trade and commerce
Defence	Ministries of defence, army, navy, air force, coast guard
Supplying internal government needs	Ministries of supply and services, Queen's printers
Finance	Ministries of finance and treasury boards
International affairs	Ministries of external or foreign affairs

Source: Hodgetts (1973).

and expansion of ministries, departments and agencies in areas such as defence, transportation and, later, social welfare, education and health provision (Derlien and Peters 2008). These kinds of organizations can be very large (the US Department of Defense, for example, has over two million employees, including approximately 650,000 civilians but not including many thousands more contractors and contract employees) and can be subdivided into hundreds of separate branches, bureaus, sections and agencies. They employ the most personnel and deliver by far the largest percentage of state-provided goods and services in liberal-democratic, and virtually all other, forms of modern government.

The 'government employees' employed in these departments are typically civil or public servants. In most liberal-democratic countries, these are unionized and well-paid positions, and although this is not the case in many other countries where officials may supplement their wages illegally through various forms of corruption ('kickbacks', bribes, 'service' payments, expediting 'fees' and so on), in either case the use of public servants to directly deliver public services is an expensive proposition, which in itself discourages its use. How well these officials are educated and trained and what kinds of facilities and information they have to work with also affect their capacity, efficiency and perceived competence and, along with cost, can play a significant role in their placement within a policy design (Brunsson 2006). Countries or sectors with well-resourced administrative systems regarded as highly efficient and competent by their citizenry are more likely to feature direct government service provision in their policy designs than countries with corrupt or inefficient civil services, given the advantages the former hold for governments in terms of cost and ease of programme administration compared to the latter.

Central support agencies

These are agencies which are similar in appearance to line departments, but often act more like private companies, delivering services within governments rather than to external constituencies. Some of these are very old (like government stationers and printers), while others (like government systems and information technology units) are much more recent. Many of these agencies are quite large, and since they often serve functions similar to private companies, they are, and have often been, primary targets for government efforts to develop market modes of governance in some sectors through contracting out or privatizing government services – that is, they are simply turned into 'firms' supplying government services by severing their funding through general appropriations revenue and establishing autonomous boards of directors and often some form of stock ownership. Cost issues are typically a major factor influencing their inclusion, or exclusion, in policy designs.

Social and health insurance and pension plans

The social and health insurance and pension schemes used in many countries for unemployment insurance, elderly income support and healthcare are other government schemes which often feature the use of organizational implementation tools. These are often bank or insurance-like financial institutions in which all individuals in certain categories are mandated to make payments to a government agency which acts, usually, as a deposit holder and a monopoly insurance provider for that group (Katzman 1988). Some of these schemes, of course, are amongst the largest areas of government expenditure and are virtually identical in organizational form to direct government department and agencies given their universal and mandated nature – with the main difference being that programme funds come from dedicated insurance payments rather than general tax revenue and in many instances these organizations are run by an arms-length governing board. These schemes are generally very high profile and targeted to very specific kinds of outputs such as payments of specific kinds and amounts based on age or on the presence of a certain health characteristic. They are often intended to be revenue-neutral, although any short-term shortfalls in these schemes typically have to be made up by governments and they may at various times collect and hold very large amounts of premiums or deposits intended to pay for future obligations. These funds also can provide very large pools of capital which governments can use to finance infrastructure and other kinds of investments or lend out to the private sector or other governments. As such, they are very popular and found throughout the world, although their exact configuration and extent of private sector involvement can vary greatly from country to country (Moss 2002). Countries which do not have such schemes typically cite reasons related to their inability to bear the ongoing costs of payments or, in some cases, a desire to avoid intruding in already existing private sector programmes providing similar kinds of insurance and payouts.

Quasi-governmental organizational forms

The second general type of government agencies have an essentially bureaucratic organizational structure and also exist largely as Weberian forms of administration – although most are structured in a more 'business-like' fashion, with fewer rules and regulations guiding their behaviour than government departments and agencies and often some form of autonomous or quasi-autonomous governance, and also very often the ability to raise funds from outside general government tax revenue. These include the following main types.

Public enterprises and other corporate forms

Public enterprises or 'state-owned enterprises' (SOEs) are the most common and well-known type of quasi-governmental substantive organizational tool. SOEs undertake or have undertaken a wide variety of tasks in many jurisdictions (see Table 3.2).

Table 3.2 provides examples of the many public enterprises used in Canada in the twentieth century, a country which has not been at the forefront of the deployment of such tools but nevertheless deployed

Table 3.2 Examples of tasks undertaken by public enterprises (Canada – twentieth century)

Task	Example (Canada, twentieth century)
Housing	Canadian Mortgage and Housing Corporation
Finance	Bank of Canada, Small Business Development Bank, Caisse de Depot et Placement de Quebec
Wartime production	Canadian Arsenals
Transportation	Canadian National Railways, Via Rail, Air Canada/ Trans-Canada Airlines, St Lawrence Seaway Co., BC Ferries, Northern Transportation Company Ltd.
Strategic industries	Atomic Energy of Canada Ltd, Petro-Canada
Communications	Canadian Broadcasting Corporation, Radio-Canada
Cultural industries	Canadian Film Development Corporation, National Film Board, National Museum Corps
Utilities	SaskTel, Hydro Quebec, Ontario Hydro, BC Hydro
Infant industries	Petrosar, Athabaska Tar Sands, Canadian Development Corporation
Sick industries	Skeena Cellulose, BC Resources Investment Corporation
Property management	British Columbia Building Corporation
Regional development	Prince Rupert Coal Corporation, DEVCO, Cape Breton Development Corp.
Lotteries and vice	BC Liquor Stores, Société des Alcools de Quebec, Casino Nova Scotia, Lotto-Canada
Local utilities	Translink, Edmonton Telephones
Marketing boards	Canada Wheat Board, British Columbia Egg and Milk Marketing Board, Freshwater Fish Marketing Board

Source: Vining and Botterell (1983).

many for many different purposes, from railways, airlines and regional development initiatives of various kinds to energy security and defence.

There are many different definitions of public enterprises, with different levels of public ownership ascribed to each. Hence, for example, in Canada, the Ontario Auditor's Act defines 'public enterprise' as

a corporation which is not an agency of the Crown and having 50 percent or more of its issued and outstanding shares vested in the government or having the appointment of a majority of its Board of directors made or approved by the Lt. Gov in Council thus including a specified level of ownership and a means of control within the definition itself (Prichard 1983).

Perry and Rainey (1988) developed an exhaustive typology of these kinds of enterprises by examining the different types of ownership, sources of funding and mode of social control exercised over these organizations. The key feature of these organizations, however, is that they are government-owned but have a corporate form and are not administrative agencies. That is, they operate under separate legislation or under general corporate legal principles, and government control is exercised indirectly as a function of government share ownership rather than through direction by a cabinet minister or agency head. Typically this control is exercized through voting control over appointments to the company board of directors, who usually can be removed 'at pleasure' by the government. The board of directors then hires and fires senior management so that government control is indirect and at 'arm's-length', unlike the more 'hands-on' management and control of direct government administrative agencies.

Some public enterprises can raise and borrow money on their own authority, while others are limited in their sphere of independence and must seek funding or permission from governments to borrow on public or international markets. Similarly, some SOEs are free to set whatever prices they would like for their products, while others must seek government permission to alter prices and may be subsidized to provide a good or service at below market value. While government share ownership can drop below 50 per cent and still exercise control if the remainder of the shares is widely held, it is more common for a government to own 50 per cent or more of voting shares (in fact, it is very common for them to own 100 per cent, sometimes through a so-called 'golden share' provision in which there is only one share issued and it is owned by the government). However, in recent years there is a growing number of 'mixed' enterprises, with joint public–private or multiple government ownership.

These companies can be exceedingly large, although they can also be much smaller, in some cases limited to one or two factories or offices. Sovereign wealth funds, holding the proceeds of oil and gas or pension revenues in countries like Singapore and Dubai, for example, are amongst the largest firms in the world in terms of assets and can control hundreds of billions of dollars in investments (Elson 2008), while large public hydroelectrical or petrochemical utilities in countries like Canada, Norway, Mexico, Iran and Venezuela also rank first amongst companies in those countries based on size of assets controlled (Laux and Molot 1988).

The use of SOEs is common in corporatist forms of governance, which prize their high levels of automaticity, intrusiveness and visibility as well as their generally low cost and ability to be precisely targeted in different sectors and policy areas and not distracted by issues in other areas as are government agencies. However, there have also been many efforts to privatize these companies, or move their ownership from the government to the private sector, as some governments have attempted to shift to more market modes of governance for ideological reasons or to cut costs (Savas 1989).

These efforts have been successful in sectors where competition exists, such as marketing boards, product producing companies and property management (Savas 1987; Laux 1993), but have generally foundered in other areas where the privatized corporation has simply become a private monopoly service provider. This has often been the case with large-scale utilities such as water, electricity or public transportation providers where natural monopoly conditions often exist which make it difficult for new entrants to compete with established companies who control, for example, bus routes, rail or water lines, and electricity generation and distribution systems. In these cases, they have often been re-nationalized or re-regulated through the creation of regulatory oversight agencies and mechanisms (Leland and Smirnova 2009).

Organizational hybrids (alternative service delivery)

In recent years, numerous hybrid forms of indirect government organizations have been developed and implemented in many jurisdictions at least in part to deal with these difficulties in privatizing government services. These have often been proposed in situations where governments would like to privatize or contract out government services but where there is not a competitive market, thereby limiting the utility of outright sale or divestment by a government.

Examples of these types of tools include the so-called 'special operating agencies' (SOAs) (Koppell 2003; Birrell 2008), which were established in many countries in the 1980s and 1990s in an effort to grant more autonomy to central service agencies and remove them from day-to-day government control. This was typically done by 'outsourcing' whatever services could be secured from a competitive external marketplace, while allowing agencies that provide those goods and services which could not be so relocated to charge real prices to purchasers and to retain their earnings and make their own reinvestment decisions. Such organizations were formed in many jurisdictions for example, to replace government print shops and print or travel services.

A second type of hybrid is the 'quasi-autonomous non-governmental organization' or *quango*, an organizational form in which a non-governmental agency is established and given a grant of authority by a government to provide a particular good or service (Hood 1986). These are generally more independent than standard public enterprises and can be very precisely targeted. Many airports, ports and harbours, for example, are run by such 'independent authorities' which rely on governments for their monopoly position but which are answerable to their own boards for their activities rather than to the government itself. These agencies are usually then able to charge their own prices for the goods or services they provide, retain their earnings and raise funds on capital markets for investments, removing these items from government books.

There can be serious principle-agent problems with these kinds of agencies, however, which can affect their use. Maintaining the arm's-length nature of the relationship of public enterprises and quangos to government is difficult, and such agencies may not have enough autonomy for governments to avoid the consequences of scandals or other problems associated with them as might occur, for example, with a failure of a prominent airport or harbour. That is, these relationships can be either too close (day-to-day interference) or too distant (agencies become distant and aloof powers unto themselves). Utilizing this form of substantive organizational tool can be also very expensive and linked to unpopular actions, with political and economic consequences for governments – like tax increases, political scandals and high-profile financing and operational issues such as charging excessive landing rights or baggage handling fees at airports or reserving choice landing and boarding locations for preferred carriers. Many public agencies also do not have to face the discipline of the market in terms of meeting shareholder or investor expectations for profitability, and hence lack at least this incentive to operate in a cost-efficient manner. These kinds of visibility and cost issues generally discourage the inclusion of these agencies in policy designs outside the areas and activities listed above.

Partnerships, commissioning and contracting out

More recent efforts on the part of some governments to offload legal and financial responsibility for goods and service delivery and have existing goods and services delivered through the private or quasi-governmental sector – have evolved into several distinct forms of organization which are more private than public, with the public sector acting mainly as a (guaranteed) purchaser of goods and services provided by private companies (Grimshaw et al. 2001).

One typical form of such activity is 'contracting out' or outsourcing, in which internal provision of some good or service is simply replaced with a source external to government (Zarco-Jasso 2005). This can be more complicated if a non-governmental provider does not exist for a particular product or service, so that a government must first, or simultaneously, create such a provider, often by providing long-term purchase guarantees for specific products, from nuclear energy and isotopes to health services of various kinds. Outsourcing of highway and railway maintenance in many countries in the 1980s and 1990s, for example, involved government managers creating their own firms, which then bid on and received government contracts to provide maintenance services for those roads; those companies then immediately hired former government workers, and in some cases used former government equipment, to provide the same service provided by the government in the pre-contract era. The initial and expected future cost savings governments expected to accrue through this process provided the impetus for this form of activity.

More recently, this form of activity moved from the service to the capital goods sector with the development of the so-called 'P3s' or 'public-private partnerships' in which governments encourage private sector firms to build and operate public infrastructure such as schools, office buildings, hospitals and sports facilities, and even transportation infrastructure such as bridges and roads, in return for a government guarantee of a long-term lease or use agreement with the provider. The net effect of this activity is to remove capital costs from government budgets while retaining the service (Rosenau 1999). Different kinds of these partnerships exist, such as collaborative partnerships with private companies to build and operate hospitals or sports infrastructure to the use of NGOs to control hospital admissions for the disabled. Operational partnerships with companies and other governments to share costs for many of the items discussed earlier also exist as do contributory partnerships where governments may provide partnership funding without necessarily controlling the use of such funds, as occurs when matching funds are provided by more senior government for local- or community-based environmental improvement projects and programmes.

Although popular in some countries and sectors in recent years as examples of 'collaborative' or 'joined-up' government, such schemes often stretch the resources of non-profit or volunteer organizations and can result in inefficient or incompetent delivery of goods and services (Riccucci and Meyers 2008). Problems with private sector partners encountering financial problems with PPP contracts or their other activities jeopardizing a PPP project have also led to high profile failures and government take-overs of contracts in mid-stream. These kinds of cost and reliability issues have increasingly affected considerations of such tools and restricted their inclusion in policy designs.

Commissioning

Commissioning is the most recently recognized collaborative technique which, as Taylor and Migone (2017) put it:

> Generally refers to a more strategic and dynamic approach to public service design and delivery with a clear focus on aligning resources to desired outcomes and by injecting greater diversity and competition into the public service economy. By creating public service markets, the expertise and resources of the private and not-for-profit sectors can be harnessed and leveraged through new business and delivery models.

Commissioning goes well beyond traditional procurement and outsourcing agendas with the aim of increasing service levels from both private and community partners by involving 'third sector' actors, such as NGOs, in both service target formulation and design ('co-design') and service delivery ('co-management'). The provision of stable funding and the ongoing interactions with government funding agencies, it is argued, allow the capacity of third-sector actors to be enhanced at the same time that co-design and co-management ensure that outcomes match the expectations of clients rather than agencies (Bovaird et al. 2014).

Commissioning suffers from many of the same NGO capacity issues raised above, however. Again, as Taylor and Migone (2017) note:

> This means that the various organizations involved redefine their relations with the public administration on one level, with the clients/users of the services on another and finally with each other. A critical element in this relationship is the creation of high level trust relations among the stakeholders. This trust will affect the flow of information and help in the creation of a contestable environment where multiple parties can move away from hindrances to outcome-based approaches such as overly legalistic contracts, enable the devolution of meaningful autonomy to those who are ultimately accountable and responsible for the delivery of services.

As they note, however, in some cases, the new relationship will modify established sets of interactions, such as when increased competitiveness of non-profit organizations results in decreased cooperation amongst the providers or when service provision becomes the central focus of NGO activity, replacing other kinds of membership activity, including those devoted to recruitment and retention of members.

Contracting

Contracting is probably the most well-known organization-based activity which involves government. All government contract for services of course, from provision of military equipment to office stationary. However in recent years many efforts have been made to reduce the level of direct state involvement in the provision of public services and the number of government personnel deployed to do so, through the replacement of civil servants and internal procurement processes with contractual arrangements with, usually, non-governmental organizations, primarily private businesses (Vincent Jones 2006). Various forms of contracting out exist, such as the PPPs or public-private partnerships discussed earlier. However other less rigorous forms of contracting exist in areas such as healthcare, education and prisons, in which contracts may not involve large investments and profit sharing, but rather simply remove major expenditure areas, such as penitentiaries, or minor ones such as janitorial services, from government books, budgets and payrolls (Roehrich et al. 2014; Thadani 2014). These activities are often undertaken in order to avoid sub-optimal production of services by relatively expensive government workers and also to avoid payments of benefits and superannuation to civil servants.

In the case of contracting, however, many supporters of the concept have noted significant limitations which can prevent contracting from functioning effectively. The 2016 Nobel Prize in Economics, for example, was awarded to two economists who specialize in detailing the significant flaws and limits of contracting in areas such as prisons and healthcare (Holmstrom and Milgrom 1991). Their concern was with the difficulty encountered by governments in enforcing quality control in such contracts when the nature of the service provided (i.e. its quality) was dependent on difficult-to-monitor interactions between, for example, patients and doctors or prisoners and prison guards. These and other criticisms highlight the need to carefully negotiate realistic contracts and deal with the information asymmetries and knowledge gaps linked to public services, as well as other issues such as difficulties encountered in cancelling contracts or preventing contractees from simply reneging on their contracted obligations.

Non-state and society-based tools: co-production and certification

Efforts at policy reform around substantive organizational tools have been omnipresent in many developed and developing countries over the past several decades and have often featured efforts to reduce the number of state-based tools and shift their activities either towards hybrid instruments or, in some cases, away from state-based organizations altogether. Many of these efforts have featured waves of management reforms and administrative re-structuring, including privatizations, de-regulation and re-regulation and the other activities cited above (Ramesh and Howlett 2006). These efforts have also led to the articulation and promotion of several alternative modes of governing to more traditional 'hierarchical' or state-led ones which still nevertheless include governments as key organizational actors.

Many of these techniques are 'market-based' and constitute efforts to replace government activity with private sector actions. However, others are focused less on zero-sum notions of state-market relations, but include more complex ideas about involving 'civil society' actors more directly in 'collaborative' policy-making, administration and implementation (Brudney 1987). These kinds of activities come in many forms, but two which have received a great deal of attention in recent years are 'co-production' and 'certification'.

Certification

Certification is a term used to capture the activities of many non-state actors involved in areas such as forestry, fisheries, organizing foods and other similar areas in which quality control and enforcement of standards are accomplished less directly than is the case with traditional government supplied command and control regulation and government agencies (Cashore et al. 2004). In these cases, for a variety of reasons, from cost to ideology, 'certification' of standards is undertaken by civil society organizations, such as the Forestry Stewardship Council or the Marine Stewardship Council, which lack the formal authority to compel business and industries to abide by regulatory standards but which utilize (often negative) publicity, boycotts and other actions to encourage compliance of firms with set standards of behaviour, from netsize and type in the case of the fishery to sustainable logging practices in the forest sector.

These tools are often referred to as non-state market-based (NSMD) tools (Cashore 2002) since they do not rely upon state authority for their power and legitimacy to regulate private sector activity, but rather do so through market activities such as product labelling and producer certifications which affect consumer behaviour and preferences, for example, for organic produce or sustainably harvested timber, fish or coffee, amongst others. It is debatable, however, if these kinds of efforts could work without the 'iron-fist' of a threat of government regulation lurking in the background.

It is also the case that such schemes rely heavily on the reputation of the certifier for honesty, accuracy and precision. Certification only functions effectively if trust exists between the public and the certifiers and between the certifiers and the certified companies and governments. Concerns about second-class regulation or corrupt standards can easily undermine years of work building up a certified brand. Similarly, competing or dueling certifiers can also undermine existing schemes and impede their effectiveness. If their reputation is damaged, as has happened from time to time with products such as wine or olives in which additives were added or cheaper products substituted for expected ones, such schemes can collapse and require either substantial reform or government takeover, revealing their dependence on government organizations, ultimately, to serve as the guarantor of quality.

Co-production

Co-production is a short-hand term for a variety of governance arrangements which involve citizens in the production and delivery of public services, some of which have already been discussed above, such as 'co-design' or 'co-management' (Brandsen and Honingh 2016). In the USA, these ideas generated interest amongst public administration scholars in the 1970s and the 1980s in areas such as storefront policing, and experienced a revival in the decades after the turn-of-the-century in many areas from education to environmental protection and highway beautification and litter control (Pestoff et al. 2006).

Originally, co-production was narrowly defined as the 'involvement of citizens, clients, consumers, volunteers and/or community organizations in producing public services as well as consuming or otherwise benefiting from them' (Alford 1998: 128). Many governance arrangements, even those thought to be purely hierarchical, such as public schooling and policing, in fact combine aspects of hierarchical or state-based governance with elements of civil society mobilization in the form of activities such as neighbourhood watches or parent-teacher associations. This involvement is often voluntary, meaning it existed as a positive externality, reducing production and delivery costs of public services. This made it very attractive to governments seeking cost reductions in public service delivery, especially ones favourable to notions of 'social enterprise' and enhanced community participation as an end- or good-in-itself (Parks et al. 1981).

Like all other tools, however, co-production also has a downside as a policy tool. In the case of co-production, it has long been recognized that expectations of free labour from co-producers may not materialize (Sorrentino et al. 2018), and schemes to incentivize co-producers through payments are susceptible to all of the usual harms of public expenditures, including corruption, clientelism and goal displacement, amongst others (Howlett et al. 2017).

Procedural organizational instruments

Substantive tools, of course, are only one of the uses towards which governmental and non-governmental organizational resources can be put. The second use is procedural. This involves the use of the organizational resources such as personnel, staffing, institutionalization and internal procedures to alter or affect policy processes in order to better achieve general government aims or specific programme activities.

It bears repeating that these tools do not involve direct or indirect goods and service delivery, as do their substantive counterparts, but rather affect process-related activities; generally efforts aimed at creating or re-structuring policy community structure and/or behaviour through government leadership or 'network management' efforts.

In any policy process, policy managers need to work with the structure and operation of any network which already exists in the area; recognize potential new actors, limit the role of ineffective actors; balance their time and resource commitments (money, technology, expertise, etc.); maintain the focus of the network in achieving goals and build trust between actors/reduce possible conflicts (Mandell 1994). In order to achieve these ends, various kinds of organizational network management tools can be used.

The key dimensions or tasks involved in the use of organizational tools for these kinds of network management activities include the identification of potentially compatible network actors, given the issue at hand; limiting potential conflicts that would hinder flexibility; recognizing legal requirements; balancing political objectives/conflicts with policy objectives and assigning costs in implementation.

Several of the most common of these tools are described in the following section.

Network management tools

There are many different types of procedural tools linked with the use of specific government organizational resources which can affect various aspects of policy subsystem behaviour in policy processes. Interest in these tools has grown as many governments have moved in the direction of more overt network management in many sectors in recent years, often in the effort to encourage NGO formation or lead their activities in certain directions rather than others.

Staff or central (executive) agencies

This is an old form of government organization, one in which a small, coordinating government agency, rather than one which directly delivers services to the public, is created to centralize and control agency initiatives in some area. Such 'staff' or 'central' agencies, unlike 'line' departments are generally created as a means to direct other administrative agencies and are often linked very closely to the political executive (Bernier et al. 2005). In Westminster-style parliamentary systems, for example, older examples include Privy Council offices and treasury board secretariats, while newer ones include presidential, premier and prime minister's offices, ministries of state, communication units, intergovernmental secretariats and various kinds of implementation units.

Although small (even most prime ministers' offices until recently had less than 100 personnel, most of whom handled correspondence), these are units which exercise a great deal of control over other bureaucratic agencies through their links to the executive and to the budgetary and policy processes in government. They have seen much growth in recent years as political executives have sought to re-establish control over far-flung administrative apparatuses (Weller et al. 1997).

Unlike line departments, these staff or central agencies are flat, or non-hierarchical, organizations typically staffed by one or two levels of political appointees, although others employ permanent officials as well. Key officials are chiefs of staff, principle secretaries and specialized positions such as a clerk of the Privy Council or cabinet secretary. These agencies play a major and increasing role in designing and coordinating policies and policy-making, ensuring accountability to legislatures and controlling the budgets, activities and plans of line departments and ministries. Their small cost is a major design consideration, although this is often offset by their high visibility and high level of intrusiveness in the affairs of the government agencies they control or coordinate which often do not like the additional level of approvals they represent for their proposals, budgets and programmes.

Tribunals and other quasi-judicial bodies

These are a second type of tool created by statute which perform many administrative functions, hearing appeals concerning licencing (e.g. of pesticides), certification (of personnel or programmes) and permits (e.g. for disposal of effluents). Appointed by government, they usually represent, or purport to represent, some diversity of interests and expertise in complex technical, legal or political issue areas. In the framework of administration, tribunals are directed toward securing compliance with administrative edicts and the achievement of identified standards of behaviour by both governmental and non-governmental actors.

Administrative hearings are conducted by tribunals in a quasi-judicial fashion, often in order to aid the tribunal in its activities. These hearings are bound by rules of natural justice, and procedures may also be dictated by statutory provisions. The decisions of tribunals are designed to be binding on the ministry in question, but may be subject to various political, administrative and judicial appeals. Public hearings may be statutorily defined as a component of the administrative process.

Tribunals often act as a mechanism with which to appeal administrative decisions, but, in most cases, proceedings are held at the discretion of a decision-making authority and public hearings are often 'after the fact' public information sessions rather than being true consultative devices (Fitzpatrick and Sinclair 2003). They can be precisely targeted and are an important component of legal modes of governance which are generally low cost and nearly invisible.

Creating or reorganizing government agencies

Another fairly commonly used procedural organizational tool is to establish new government agencies or reform existing institutions in order to focus or re-focus state and societal activities on specific problems or issue areas (Durant 2008). Setting up a new government ministry for technology or a new research council to promote advanced technologies like biotechnology, e-technologies or other high technology sectors, for example, is a common action on the part of governments wanting to target a new area of activity for further development and identify and co-ordinate the societal actors and businesses already involved in it. However, such actions are highly visible and, if repeated too often, quite costly. They are also quite intrusive and, as a result, are proposed, and used, only infrequently.

Establishing analytical units

It is more common for governments to set up internal think tanks or research institutes in order to provide policy advice to governments (Phidd 1975), many of which can perform many of the same kinds of network activities which would a new ministry or agency, but at much less cost and with less difficulty involved in their budgeting and establishment. Many government departments and agencies, for example, have established specialized policy units designed to generate studies and reports which can influence or help persuade both government officials and non-governmental actors of the merits of government plans. These agencies also often employ outside consultants to bring additional expertise and knowledge to policy formation, implementation and evaluation (Speers 2007). The knowledge they generate is used to inform internal policy-making processes and also to garner support for government positions from outside groups.

New analytical units such as those policy shops created in many jurisdictions in the 1970s and 1980s in order to promote formal policy analysis and what is now referred to as 'knowledge-based' or 'evidence-based' policy-making are good examples of the use of this kind of procedural organizational tool (Prince 1979). These agencies can be precisely targeted and are generally low cost and have low visibility. However, their impact on policy-making can raise the ire of stakeholders and others who can find them to be rivals for government knowledge and attention. Such considerations have dampened enthusiasm for such units in many jurisdictions and sectors and reduced their appeal in policy designs in recent years.

Establishing clientele units

New administrative units in areas like urban affairs, science and technology flourished in many countries in the 1970s, as did new environmental units in most countries in the 1970s and 1980s. These were joined by units dealing with areas such as youth and small business in the 1990s; and in the post-1990 period, other new units were developed in countries like New Zealand, Canada and Australia to deal with aboriginal affairs, and promote bi- or multiculturalism, women's rights and human rights. Human rights units dealing with minorities and the disabled are good examples of network mobilization and activation occasioned by government organizational (re)engineering which raised the prominence of these issues with governments and the public and led to many new laws and initiatives in the years following their creation (Malloy 1999).

Table 3.3 Analytical agency network managerial tasks

1. Vertical and horizontal coordination
2. Overcome institutional blockages like federalism and divisions of power
3. 'Mainstreaming'
4. Building commitments
5. Building legitimacy/developing visions and agreement on alternatives
6. Building coalitions
7. Structuring NGO activity, e.g. lobbying activities

Source: Mandell (2000).

In general, these agencies can be precisely targeted in order to undertake the management functions shown in Table 3.3. They are very popular given their generally low cost and high visibility and effectiveness.

Establishing government reviews, ad hoc task forces, commissions, inquiries and public hearings

A sixth common procedural organizational tool used by governments is the establishment of a government review. These range from formal, mandated, periodic reviews of legislation and government activity by congressional or parliamentary committees and internal administrative bodies to 'ad hoc' processes such as task forces or enquiries designed to activate or mobilize network actors to support government initiatives or investigate accidents or malfeasance of various kinds, often related to judicial or administrative conduct (Marchildon 2007).

Ad hoc task forces and enquiries are typically temporary bodies, much shorter term and often more issue-related than institutionalized advisory committees. Ad hoc commissions are created as instruments to consult a variety of interests with regard to economic and other areas of planning activity. These range from the presidential or royal commissions to those created at the departmental level.

Task forces have been created in many jurisdictions for planning, consultation or conflict resolution concerning many specific issues. The task force may be invoked by a government when there is an area of conflict in which different groups have different interests and perspectives or where they require information in order to arrive at a decision or judgement.

The subject matter of an ad hoc commission is typically urgent, of concern to more than one ministry and level of government, and is the subject of some controversy. They are invoked at the discretion of government and are subject to political, economic and social pressures. Indeed, the very initiation of the commission is likely to be the product of pressure by public interest groups (Chapman 1973). Employment of these instruments for this purpose can result in serious legitimation problems for governments utilizing these policy tools, however, given their high level of visibility (Sulitzeanu-Kenan 2007). Presidential and royal commissions are the most formal and arm's-length and, therefore, are the most difficult for governments to control and predict, and hence are used less often.

Public participation through hearings is the most common type of public or network consultation in many sectors. Hearings vary by degree of formalization and by when they occur in a policy process. The most effective and influential are often flexible processes that are geared towards policy formulation such as project reviews or environmental assessments, but the most common are rigid processes that take place in or after the implementation stage of a process, such as a formal policy evaluation exercise (Dion 1973). Public hearings are often mandated by legislation and most often occur after a decision has been taken – that is, purely as information and/or legitimation devices. Actual instances of open, truly empowered public hearing processes are rare (Rowe and Frewer 2005).

Although sometimes used for other purposes such as information collection or blame attribution, these tools are often also used to overcome institutional 'blockages' and veto points such as those which are commonly found in federal–state or intergovernmental relations or in interdepartmental jurisdictional struggles. They can also help bolster the capacity of groups to become more involved in the policy process if funding is extended to their participants, thereby promoting network governance. They can be precisely targeted and are generally low cost. However, their high level of visibility can cause problems for governments and results in their less frequent appearance in policy designs than would otherwise be the case (Rowe and Frewer 2006).

Legislative and executive oversight agencies

This category of procedural organizational tools includes specialized agencies with very different policy-making functions, like arm's-length independent auditor-generals or access to information commissioners. These are units typically attached to legislatures, providing some oversight or control over executive branch activities. Many principle-agent problems can be overcome through administrative procedures mandating oversight agency reviews of government actions, especially if these are linked to funding and budgetary issues (McCubbins and Lupia 1994) and most governments have many such oversight bodies, a phenomenon which itself can create problems with different investigations and reports targeting the same issues and problems, sometimes with different conclusions and recommendations.

Conclusion: organizational tools – the forgotten fundamental in policy design studies

Practical experience and ideological predilections have shaped the substance of much of the debate on the use of the organizational resources of government, with initiatives ranging from preferences for democracy, popular participation and collaboration to concerns about budget deficits and public sector inefficiencies in hierarchy-based systems leading to similar efforts to modify or restrict the use of organizational tools. In recent years, a strong preference for shifts towards non-hierarchical forms of governance, coupled with discontent with the results of market-based reforms in the 1970s to 1990s, has led to increasing attention being paid to more civil-society or networked forms of 'collaborative governance'.

It is true that organization-based implementation tools are generally costly and have high visibility. This is because they rely on government personnel funded by appropriations from general revenue raised through taxes or royalties (although some are also funded from market revenue stemming from the sale of goods or services). The use of tax-based funding makes the use of public servants expensive in the sense that governments tend to have a limited capacity to tax citizens to pay for services and incur opportunity costs no matter which activity they choose to adopt. It can also lead to governance failures, as the link between system outputs and inputs (expenditures and revenues) is usually not clear, providing the opportunity for funds to be misallocated and effort misspent, all in the fishbowl environment of public government.

Despite their real or perceived cost, and in spite of many efforts to create or replace them with other forms of service and goods delivery, as noted at the outset of this chapter, direct delivery of goods and services by public agencies remains the 'forgotten fundamental' of implementation instruments and policy designs. 'Old-fashioned' government agencies and line departments are still the most common and pervasive policy instruments in most sectors. Even in the ostensibly most private sector-oriented market governance systems (like the USA or, more recently, New Zealand), direct government goods and service production usually reaches close to 50 per cent of gross national product (GNP) – that is, half of the dollar value of all goods and services produced in a country in one year – while direct civil service employment typically hovers in the area of 15–20 per cent of the labour force, but can also be much higher (Christensen and Pallesen 2008).

This organizational activity is somewhat sectorally focused, due to large publicly provided expenditures on direct government activities like the defence and the military which cannot be delivered by the private sector, and/or items such as healthcare, social security, education and pensions associated with the development of modern welfare states and the extension of legal rights to these services to members of the public. It also includes what statistical agencies refer to as the 'MUSH' sector – municipalities, universities, schools and hospitals – which, in many countries, are established as autonomous or semi-autonomous operating agencies of more senior levels of government. In many countries, MUSH sector agencies are amongst the largest employers since the activities they undertake – such as education and healthcare, as well as sewer, road and parks maintenance – are very labour-intensive. Many of the recent innovations in organizational forms, ranging from special operating agencies, to quangos, private-public partnerships and various kinds of hybrid organizations, have emerged largely in the effort to reduce the size of these existing organizations.

This has promoted the frequent appearance of experiments in alternate instruments and policy designs, although much less often in their realization in practice. Lost in the identification of alternative forms of organizational tools and service delivery by governments around the world in a variety of sectors has been the understanding of exactly what kind of governance arrangement is 'collaborative', and especially under what conditions a preferred governance mode could actually address a particular sector's problems. Given that all collaborative modes are vulnerable to specific kinds of failures due to inherent vulnerabilities when governments reform or try to shift from one mode to the other modes, policy-makers need to understand not only the nature of the problem they are trying to address and the skills and resources they have at their disposal to address it, but especially the innate features of each potential alternative mode and the capabilities and competences each requires in order to operate at a high level of performance.

Notwithstanding this, significant areas of public expenditure and efforts, such as healthcare and education, have generally proved immune to privatization efforts given their overall cost structures, mandatory service delivery nature and high levels of citizen support. Most successes have come in either small-scale direct service privatizations or in single-industry company privatizations which have generally not significantly altered earlier tool uses (Verhoest et al. 2012).

Procedural organizational instruments have also been growing in frequency of appearance, but for different reasons. Government reorganizations are increasingly common, and these reorganizations and the new agencies often created alongside them are intended to use government organizational resources to re-focus government efforts and interactions with policy community/network members rather than directly improve the delivery of particular types of goods and services (Peters 1992). The reorganization of existing departments and agencies serves to re-position government administration within policy networks, often inserting government actors between competing private actors in networks by, for example, creating consumer departments to sit between producers and (un)organized consumers (Bache 2010). These moves are often accompanied by the increasing use of government reviews and inquiries, as well as consultative conferences and other similar organizational forms for stakeholder and public consultation, resulting in different mixes of these fundamental tools in contemporary policy designs than in the past.

References

Albrow, Martin. *Bureaucracy.* New York: Praeger Publishers, 1970.

Alford, John. "A Public Management Road Less Travelled: Clients as Co-producers of Public Services." *Australian Journal of Public Administration* 57, no. 4 (December 1, 1998): 128–37.

Bache, Ian. "Partnership as an EU Policy Instrument: A Political History." *West European Politics* 33, no. 1 (January 2010): 58–74.

Bernier, Luc. "The Future of Public Enterprises: Perspectives from the Canadian Experience." *Annals of Public and Cooperative Economics* 82, no. 4 (December 1, 2011): 399–419.

Bernier, Luc, Keith Brownsey, and Michael Howlett, eds. *Executive Styles in Canada: Cabinet Structures and Leadership Practices in Canadian Government.* Toronto, ON: University of Toronto Press, 2005.

Birrell, Derek. "Devolution and Quangos in the United Kingdom: The Implementation of Principles and Policies for Rationalisation and Democratisation." *Policy Studies* 29, no. 1 (2008): 35–49.

Bovaird, Tony, Ian Briggs, and Martin Willis. "Strategic Commissioning in the UK: Service Improvement Cycle or Just Going Round in Circles?" *Local Government Studies* 40, no. 4 (July 4, 2014): 533–59.

Brandsen, Taco, and Marlies Honingh. "Distinguishing Different Types of Coproduction: A Conceptual Analysis Based on the Classical Definitions." *Public Administration Review* 76, no. 3 (2016): 427–35.

Brudney, Jeffrey L. "Coproduction and Privatization: Exploring the Relationship and Its Implications." *Nonprofit and Voluntary Sector Quarterly* 16, no. 3 (July 1, 1987): 11–21.

Brunsson, Nils. *Mechanisms of Hope: Maintaining the Dream of the Rational Organization.* Copenhagen Business School Press, 2006.

Cashore, Benjamin. "Legitimacy and the Privatization of Environmental Governance: How Non-State Market-Driven (NSMD) Governance Systems Gain Rule-Making Authority." *Governance* 15, no. 4 (2002): 503–29.

Cashore, Benjamin, Graeme Auld, and Deanna Newsom. *Governing Through Markets: Forest Certification and the Emergence of Non-State Authority.* New Haven, CT: Yale University Press, 2004.

Chapman, Richard A. *The Role of Commissions in Policy-Making.* London: George Allen and Unwin, 1973.

Christensen, Jorgen Gronnegaard, and Thomas Pallesen. "Public Employment Trends and the Organization of Public Sector Tasks." In *The State at Work, Volume 2: Comparative Public Service Systems,* edited by Hand-Ulrich Derlien and Peters B. Guy. Cheltenham: Edward Elgar, 2008.

Derlien, Hans-Ulrich, and Peters B. Guy, eds. *The State at Work, Volume 1: Public Sector Employment in 10 Countries.* Cheltenham: Edward Elgar, 2008.

Dion, L. "The Politics of Consultation." *Government and Opposition* 8, no. 3 (1973): 332–53.

Durant, Robert F. "Sharpening a Knife Cleverly: Organizational Change, Policy Paradox, and the 'Weaponizing' of Administrative Reform." *Public Administration Review* 68, no. 2 (2008): 282–94.

Elson, Anthony. "The Sovereign Wealth Funds of Singapore." *World Economics* 9, no. 3 (2008): 73–96.

Fitzpatrick, Patricia, and A. John Sinclair. "Learning through Public Involvement in Environmental Assessment Hearings." *Journal of Environmental Management* 67, no. 2 (February 2003): 161–74.

Grimshaw, D., S. Vincent, and H. Willmott. "New Control Modes and Emergent Organizational Forms: Private-Public Contracting in Public Administration." *Administrative Theory and Practice* 23, no. 3 (2001): 407–30.

Hodgetts, J. E. *The Canadian Public Service: A Physiology of Government 1867–1970.* Toronto, ON: University of Toronto Press, 1973.

Holmstrom, Bengt, and Paul Milgrom. "Multitask Principal–Agent Analyses: Incentive Contracts, Asset Ownership, and Job Design." *The Journal of Law, Economics, and Organization* 7, no. special_issue (1991): 24–52.

Hood, C. "The Hidden Public Sector: The 'Quangocratization' of the World?" In *Guidance, Control, and Evaluation in the Public Sector,* edited by F. X. Kaufman, G. Majone, and V. Ostrom, 183–207. Berlin: Walter de Gruyter, 1986.

Howlett, Michael, Anka Kekez, and Ora-ORN Poocharoen. "Understanding Co-Production as a Policy Tool: Integrating New Public Governance and Comparative Policy Theory." *Journal of Comparative Policy Analysis: Research and Practice* 19, no. 5 (October 20, 2017): 487–501.

Katzman, M. T. "Societal Risk Management through the Insurance Market." In *Market-Based Public Policy,* edited by R. C. Hula, 21–42. London: Macmillan, 1988.

58   *Policy tools*

Koppell, Jonathan G. S. *The Politics of Quasi-Government: Hybrid Organizations and the Dynamics of Bureaucratic Control.* Cambridge: Cambridge University Press, 2003.

Laux, J. "How Private Is Privatization." *Canadian Public Policy* 19, no. 4 (1993): 398–411.

Laux, J. K., and M. A. Molot. *State Capitalism: Public Enterprise in Canada.* Ithaca, NY: Cornell University Press, 1988.

Leland, Suzanne, and Olga Smirnova. "Reassessing Privatization Strategies 25 Years Later: Revisting Perry and Babitsky's Comparative Performance Study of Urban Bus Transit Services." *Public Administration Review* 69, no. 5 (2009): 855–67.

Leman, C. K. "The Forgotten Fundamental: Successes and Excesses of Direct Government." In *Beyond Privatization: The Tools of Government Action*, edited by L. M. Salamon, 51–92. Washington, DC: Urban Institute, 1989.

Leman, C. K., and L. M. Salamon. "Direct Government." In *The Tools of Government: A Guide to the New Governance*, 48–79. New York: Oxford University Press, 2002.

Malloy, J. "What Makes a State Advocacy Structure Effective? Conflicts between Bureaucratic and Social Movements Criteria." *Governance* 12, no. 3 (1999): 267–88.

Mandell, M. P. "Managing Interdependencies through Program Structures: A Revised Paradigm." *The American Review of Public Administration* 25, no. 1 (1994): 99–121.

Mandell, M. P. 'A Revised Look at Management in Network Structures'. *International Journal of Organizational Theory and Behavior* 3, nos.1/2 (2000): 185–210.

Marchildon, Gregory F. "Royal Commissions and the Policy Cycle in Canada: The Case of Health Care." In *Political Leadership and Representation in Canada*, edited by Hans J. Michelmann, Donald C. Story, and Jeffreu S. Steeves. Toronto, ON: University of Toronto Press, 2007.

McCubbins, M. D., and A. Lupia. "Learning from Oversight: Fire Alarms and Police Patrols Reconstructed." *Journal of Law, Economics and Organization* 10, no. 1 (1994): 96–125.

Moss, David A. *When All Else Fails: Government as the Ultimate Risk Manager.* Cambridge, MA: Harvard University Press, 2002.

Parks, Roger B., Paula C. Baker, Larry Kiser, Ronald Oakerson, Elinor Ostrom, Vincent Ostrom, Stephen L Percy, Martha B Vandivort, Gordon P Whitaker, and Rick Wilson. "Consumers as Coproducers of Public Services: Some Economic and Institutional Considerations." *Policy Studies Journal* 9, no. 7 (June 1, 1981): 1001–11.

Perry, James L., and Hal G. Rainey. "The Public-Private Distinction in Organization Theory: A Critique and Research Strategy." *Academy of Management Review* 13, no. 2 (1988): 182–201.

Pestoff, Victor, Stephen P. Osborne, and Taco Brandsen. "Patterns of Co-Production in Public Services." *Public Management Review* 8 (December 2006): 591–95.

Peters, B. G. "Government Reorganization: A Theoretical Analysis." *International Political Science Review* 13, no. 2 (1992): 199–218.

Phidd, R. W. "The Economic Council of Canada: Its Establishment, Structure, and Role in the Canadian Policy-Making System 1963–74." *Canadian Public Administration* 18, no. 3 (1975): 428–73.

Prichard, J. R. S. *Crown Corporations in Canada: The Calculus of Instrument Choice.* Toronto, ON: Butterworths, 1983.

Prince, M. J. "Policy Advisory Groups in Government Departments." In *Public Policy in Canada: Organization, Process, Management,* edited by G. B. Doern and P. Aucoin, 275–300. Toronto, ON: Gage, 1979.

Ramesh, M., and M. Howlett. *Deregulation and Its Discontents: Rewriting the Rules in Asia.* Aldershot: Edward Elgar, 2006.

Riccucci, Norma M., and Marcia K. Meyers. "Comparing Welfare Service Delivery among Public, Nonprofit and For-Profit Work Agencies." *International Journal of Public Administration* 31 (2008): 1441–54.

Roehrich, Jens K., Michael A. Lewis, and Gerard George (2014). "Are Public–Private Partnerships a Healthy Option? A Systematic Literature Review of 'Constructive' Partnerships between Public and Private Actors." *Social Science & Medicine* 113: 110–19.

Rosenau, P. V. "The Strengths and Weaknesses of Public-Private Policy Partnerships." *American Behavioral Scientist* 43, no. 1 (1999): 10–34.

Rowe, Gene, and Lynn J. Frewer. "A Typology of Public Engagement Mechanisms." *Science, Technology & Human Values* 30, no. 2 (April 1, 2005): 251–90.

Rowe, Mike, and Laura McAllister. "The Roles of Commissions of Inquiry in the Policy Process." *Public Policy and Administration* 21, no. 4 (December 1, 2006): 99–115.

Rudolph, L., and S. Rudolph. "Authority and Power in Bureaucratic and Patrimonial Bureaucracy." *World Politics* 31, no. 2 (1979): 195–227.

Savas, E. S. *Privatization: The Key to Better Government.* Chatham: Chatham House Publishers, 1987.

Savas, E. S. "A Taxonomy of Privatization Strategies." *Policy Studies Journal* 18, no. 2★Copy on file (1989): 343–55.

Sorrentino, Maddalena, Mariafrancesca Sicilia, and Michael Howlett. "Understanding Co-Production as a New Public Governance Tool." *Policy and Society* 37, no. 3 (July 3, 2018): 277–93.

Speers, Kimberly. "The Invisible Public Service: Consultants and Public Policy in Canada." In *Policy Analysis in Canada: The State of the Art,* edited by L. Dobuzinskis, M. Howlett, and D. Laycock, 220–31. Toronto, ON: University of Toronto Press, 2007.

Sulitzeanu-Kenan, R. "Scything the Grass: Agenda-Setting Consequences of Appointing Public Inquiries in the UK, A Longnitudinal Analysis." *Policy and Politics* 35, no. 4 (2007): 629–50.

Taylor, Robert, and Andrea Migone. "From Procurement to the Commissioning of Public Services." IPAC, Charlottetown, 2017.

Thadani, Khushbu B. "Public Private Partnership in the Health Sector: Boon or Bane." *Procedia - Social and Behavioral Sciences* 157 (November 27, 2014): 307–16. doi:10.1016/j.sbspro.2014.11.033.

Verhoest, Koen, Sandra Van Thiel, Geert Bouckaert, and Per Laegreid, eds. *Government Agencies: Practices and Lessons from 30 Countries*. Basingstoke: Palgrave Macmillan, 2012.

Vincent-Jones, Peter. *The New Public Contracting: Regulation, Responsiveness, Relationality*. Oxford: Oxford University Press, 2006.

Vining, A. R., and R. Botterell. "An Overview of the Origins, Growth, Size, and Functions of Provincial Crown Corporations." In *Crown Corporations: The Calculus of Instrument Choice*, edited by J. R. S. Pritchard, 303–68. Toronto, ON: Butterworths, 1983.

Voorberg, W. H., V. J. J. M. Bekkers, and L. G. Tummers. "A Systematic Review of Co-Creation and Co-Production: Embarking on the Social Innovation Journey." *Public Management Review* 17, no. 9 (October 21, 2015): 1333–57.

Weber, M. *Economy and Society Berkeley*. California: University of California Press, 1978.

Weller, P., H. Bakvis, and R. A. W. Rhodes. *The Hollow Crown: Countervailing Trends in Core Executives*. New York: St. Martin's Press, 1997.

Zarco-Jasso, Hugo. "Public-Private Partnerships: A Multidimensional Model for Contracting." *International Journal of Public Policy* 1, no. 1/2 (2005): 22–40.

4 Authoritative implementation tools

There are many types of 'authoritative' implementation instruments that, like organizational tools, are a very common part, and often a central feature, of policy designs. All involve, and rely primarily upon, the ability of governments to direct or steer targets in the directions they would prefer them to go through the use of the real or perceived threat of state-enforced sanctions or coercion. While treasure resources, discussed in the next chapter, are often used to encourage 'positive' behaviour — that is, behaviour which is aligned with government goals — authoritative actions can be used for this purpose but are often used in a 'negative' sense, that is, to prevent or discourage types of behaviour which are incongruent with government expectations (Ajzen 1991).

The use of the coercive power of the state to achieve government goals through the control or alteration of societal (and governmental) behaviour is the essence of *regulation*, the most common type of governing instrument found in this category (Mitnick 1978). With regulation, the government does not provide goods and service delivery 'directly' through the use of its organizational resources but rather allows this to occur in a controlled fashion through an intermediary — usually a private company or market enterprise, but also sometimes SOEs or, more commonly, NGOs such as churches, voluntary organizations and association, trade unions and professional bodies (Scott 2001) — while retaining the ability to control and direct those actors on a day-to-day basis, often to the minutest detail.

Substantive authoritative instruments

In general, all types of regulation involve the promulgation of more or less binding rules which circumscribe or alter the behaviour of particular target groups (Kiviniemi 1986). That is, regulation commonly involves the 'public administrative policing of a private activity with respect to a rule prescribed in the public interest' (Mitnick 1978).

These rules take various forms and include standards, permits, prohibitions and executive orders among others. Some regulations, like ones dealing with criminal behaviour, are *laws* and involve the police and judicial system in their enforcement. Most regulations, however, are *administrative edicts* created under the terms of enabling legislation and administered on a continuing basis by a government department or a specialized, quasi-judicial government agency with some level of enforcement and supervisory powers (Rosenbloom 2007). In relatively rare cases, the authority to enact, enforce or adjudicate regulations can also be delegated to non-governmental organizations in various forms of 'voluntary' or 'self-regulation'. All of these types are set out below, and their strengths and weaknesses in policy designs are described.

Direct government regulation

Although citizens may not always be aware of their presence, regulations govern the price and standards of a wide variety of goods and services they consume, as well as the quality of the water they drink and the air they breathe (Baldwin and Cave 1999). It is commonly a continuing administrative process administered through specially designated regulatory agencies (Reagan 1987) in which failure to comply with government directives typically involves a penalty, sometimes financial, but also often involving incarceration and imprisonment.

This type of instrument is often referred to as 'command and control' regulation and is very common in the social and economic spheres. Criminal law, for example, is a kind of regulatory activity, as are common laws and civil codes, which all countries have and which states develop and implement, usually relatively non-controversially (May 2002).

It is sometimes difficult for governments to 'command and control' their targets if these targets resist regulatory efforts or if a government does not have the capacity or legitimacy required to enforce their orders. As a result of these difficulties, other types of regulation exist in which rules are vaguer and the threat of penalties may be, at best, remote. These different types of regulation are discussed in the following sections.

Laws

Law is an important tool of modern government and the very basis of legal modes of governance (Ziller 2005). Several different types of laws exist, however. These include distinctions often drawn by legal scholars

Table 4.1 Six types of legal instruments

1. Statutes
2. Delegated legislation between levels of government
3. Decisions of regulatory bodies and courts
4. Contracts or treaties
5. Quasi-legislation such as tax notices and interpretative bulletins
6. Reference documents such as background papers, other legislation and standing orders

Source: Keyes (1996).

between private and public law; private, civil or tort law and common law; public, criminal and administrative law and hybrids such as class action suits which combine features of public and private law. These different types of law vary substantially in terms of what kinds of situations they can be applied to, by whom and to what effect (see *Table 4.1*).

All of these laws can be thought of as 'regulations', since all involve the creation of rules governing individual behaviour. However, in the form it is usually discussed by policy scholars, 'regulation' is typically thought of as a form of public law; although even then it can also involve criminal and individual or civil actions (Kerwin 1999).

While laws can prohibit or proscribe many kinds of behaviour (and encourage others either by implication or overtly), in order to move beyond the symbolic level, they all require a strong enforcement mechanism, which includes various forms of policing and the courts. And even here, a considerable amount of variation and discretion is possible since inspections and policing can be more or less onerous and more or less frequent, can be oriented towards responding to complaints or actively looking for transgressions ('police patrols' vs 'fire alarms') and can be focused on punishment of transgressions or prevention, in the latter case often with a strong educational component designed to persuade citizens and others to adopt modes of behaviour more congruent with government aims and objectives rather than punish them for each transgression that occurs (McCubbins and Schwartz 1984). A desire for 100 per cent compliance on the part of governments requires a high level of scrutiny, and thus some kind of ongoing, institutionalized government organization or agency: typically a line department such as a police department or some other similar administrative bureau with investigatory and policing powers.

All laws are intrusive, and many are highly visible. A significant problem with the use of laws in policy designs, however, pertains to cost and precision of targeting. With respect to the first, while passage of a law is usually not all that costly, the need for enforcement is. Laws have a low degree of automaticity, as they rely upon citizen's goodwill and perceptions of legitimacy for them to be obeyed. Inevitably, this will not ensure 100 per cent compliance and will thus require the establishment of an enforcement agency, such as the police, customs agencies, immigration patrols, coast guards and the courts. Precision of targeting is an issue since most laws have general applicability and often cannot single out specific groups or targets for differential treatment. These problems have led to the use of alternate forms of regulation expected to reduce these costs and allow for improved targeting of specific actors.

Direct departmental regulation and Independent regulatory commissions

Direct administrative implementation of legislative rules is very common in modern modes of governance. However, in the economic realm, especially, it often raises concerns about corruption, favoritism and patronage, that is, in the abuse of administrative discretion to either ease enforcement in certain cases or administer it capriciously in others. Checks on administrative discretion usually exist through the court system, whereby those who feel they have been unfairly treated can often appeal administrative decisions and seek to overturn them (Edley 1990). This can be a very time-consuming and expensive process, however, and several distinct forms of regulatory agencies with semi-independent, quasi-judicial status have been developed in order to avoid governance problems associated with direct departmental regulation.

The most well known of these is the *independent regulatory commission (IRC)*. Although some early exemplars of this instrument can be found in canal authorities in Great Britain and other European railway, highway and transportation regulatory authorities of the eighteenth and nineteenth centuries, the IRC, as it is currently known, stems mainly from concerns raised in the post-Civil War (USA) regarding unfair practices in railway transportation pricing and access. These led to the creation of an innovative organizational regulatory form in the 1887 US Pendleton Act, which established the US Interstate Commerce Commission, a quasi-judicial body operating at arms-length from government which was intended to act autonomously in the creation and enforcement of regulations and which remained in operation for over 100 years (until 1995) (Cushman 1941).

Independent regulatory commissions are 'semi-independent' administrative agencies in the sense that, as was the case with public enterprises, government control is indirect and exercised via the appointment of commissioners who are more or less difficult to remove from office (Jacobzone 2005). Wu (2008) has listed 11 aspects of their organization, staffing and function which make such agencies 'independent' (see *Table 4.2*).

Table 4.2 Requisites for regulatory agency independence

1. An independent leader
2. Exclusive licencing authority
3. Independent funding
4. Private sector regulatees
5. Little movement of staff between industry and regulator
6. Consumer offices
7. Universal service offices
8. Notice and comment decision-making
9. Rules against gifts
10. Rules against conflicts of interest
11. Post-employment rules

Source: Wu (2008).

IRCs are quasi-judicial in the sense that one of their main activities is adjudicating disputes over the interpretation and enforcement of rules – a task taken away from the courts in order to ensure that expertise in the specific activities regulated is brought to bear on a case in order to have more expert, timely and predictable results. Decisions of independent regulatory commissions are still subject to judicial review, although often this is only in terms of issues relating to procedural fairness, rather than the evidentiary basis of a decision.

IRCs are relatively inexpensive, specialized bodies that can remove a great deal of the routine regulatory burden in many areas of social and economic life from government departments and the courts, and are quite popular with governments wishing to simplify their agendas and reduce their need to supervise specific forms of social behaviour on a day-to-day basis (Wonka and Rittberger 2010). In the contemporary period, independent regulatory commissions are involved with all aspects of market behaviour, production, distribution and consumption, as well as many areas of social life. Many specialized forms of IRCs exist, such as the use of '*marketing boards*', or arm's-length regulatory bodies often staffed by elected representatives of producers and granted specific rights to control prices and/or supply in areas from chicken production to organ donations, thereby creating and enforcing pricing and supply regimes on producers (Royer 2008). This has occurred primarily in areas affected by periodic bouts of over- or under-supply and can be found in areas such as bulk agricultural commodities like wheat or milk whose supply is very sensitive to price fluctuations, and in areas such as liver and heart transplants, which are subject to chronic supply shortages (Weimer 2007). These boards typically act as rationing boards charged with allocating supply quotas and setting prices in order to smooth out supply fluctuations in the activity involved. They are very common, for example, in wartime when many goods are in short supply and rationing goods from fuel to food often is a necessity.

IRCs, like more direct government regulation, have been the subject of efforts at *deregulation*, as some governments attempted to move some sectors towards more open market modes of operation. Some high-profile privatization and deregulation in transportation, telecommunication and financial industries in many countries occurred in the 1980s and 1990s as a result of these efforts however there has been no across-the-board reduction in the use of more directive tools. Like privatization, deregulation is nowhere as widespread as claimed by both enthusiasts and critics. Even in banking, the most globalized business sector, there is little or no evidence of an overall decline of regulation, and the market and credit crises of 2008 have rather led to increased moves in a re-regulatory direction in many countries, from Iceland to the USA, as well as at the international level. Indeed, regulations have been expanded in many sectors to compensate for the loss of state control following privatization of public enterprises (Jordana and Levi-Faur 2004).

There are still some concerns about the use of this instrument in policy designs, however, linked to considerations of cost and visibility. The cost of enforcement by regulatory commissions can be quite high, depending on the availability of information, and the costs of investigation and prosecution in highly legalistic and adversarial circumstances can also be very large. Regulations also are often inflexible and do not permit the consideration of individual circumstances, and can result in decisions and outcomes not intended by the regulators. They can distort voluntary or private sector activities and promote economic inefficiencies. Price regulations and direct allocation, for example, restrict the operation of the forces of demand and supply and affect the price mechanism, thus causing sometimes unpredictable economic distortions in the market. Restrictions on entry to and exit from industrial sectors, for example, can reduce competition and thus have a negative impact on prices. Regulations can also inhibit innovation and technological progress because of the market security they afford to existing firms and the limited opportunities for experimentation they might permit. For these and other reasons, they are often labelled as overly intrusive by many firms and actors (Dyerson and Mueller 1993) and efforts to avoid them through other forms of regulation (see below) are very common, though, not always successful.

Indirect government regulation

One of these alternative forms of regulation is 'indirect regulation'. There are several different types of such regulation, however, which vary in terms of their design attributes.

Delegated professional regulation

This is a relatively rare form of regulatory activity which occurs when a government transfers its authority to licence certain practices and discipline transgressors to non-governmental or quasi-governmental bodies whose boards of directors, unlike the situation with independent regulatory commissions, they typically do not appoint (Elgie 2006). Delegated regulation typically involves legislatures passing special legislation, empowering specific groups to define their own membership and regulate their own behaviour. Brockman (1998) defines it as:

> the delegation of government regulatory functions to a quasi-public body that is officially expected to prevent or reduce both incompetence (lack of skill, knowledge or ability) and misconduct (criminal, quasi-criminal or unethical behaviour) by controlling the quality of service to the public through regulating or governing activities such as licencing or registration – often involving a disciplinary system (fines, licences, suspension or revocation) and codes of conduct/ethics, etc.

This occurs most commonly in the area of professional regulation where many governments allow professions such as doctors, lawyers, accountants, engineers, teachers, urban planners and others to control entrance to their profession and to enforce professional standards of conduct through the grant of a licencing monopoly to an organization such as a bar association, a college of physicians and surgeons or a teachers' college (Tuohy and Wolfson 1978).

The idea behind delegated regulation, as with independent regulatory commissions, is that direct regulation through government departments and the courts is too expensive and time-consuming to justify the effort involved and the results achieved. Rather than tie up administrators and judges with many thousands of cases resulting from, for example, professional licencing or judicial or medical malpractice, these activities can be delegated to bodies composed of representatives of the professional field involved, who are the ones most knowledgeable about best practices and requirements in their field. Governments have neither the time nor expertise required to regulate multiple interactions between lawyers and their clients, teachers and students or doctors and patients, for example, and a form of 'self-regulation' is more practical and cost-efficient (Kuhlmann and Allsop 2008).

Scandal in areas such as business accounting in many countries in recent years, however, can undermine confidence in a profession's ability or even willingness to police itself, and can lead to a crisis in confidence in many aspects of delegated self-regulation (Tallontire 2007). Of course, any delegation of government regulatory authority can be revoked if misbehaviour ensues.

Voluntary or incentive regulation

A second form of indirect or 'self-regulation' has a more recent history than delegated regulation, and has been extended to many more areas of social and economic life. This is typically a form found in market governance systems in which, rather than establish an agency with the authority to unilaterally direct targets to follow some course of action with the ability to sanction those actors who fail to comply, a government tries to persuade targets to voluntarily adopt or conform to government aims and objectives.

Although these efforts, like certification, often exist 'under the shadow of hierarchy' (Heritier and Lehmkuhl 2008) – that is, where a real threat of enhanced oversight exists should voluntary means prove insufficient to motivate actors to alter their behaviour in the desired fashion – they also exist in realms where hierarchies don't exist, such as the international realm when a strong treaty regime, for example, cannot be agreed upon. A major advantage often cited for the use of voluntary standard-setting is cost savings, since governments do not have to pay for the creation, administration, enforcement and renewal of such standards, as would be the case with traditional command and control regulation whether implemented by departments or independent regulatory commissions. Such programmes can also be effective in international settings, where establishment of effective legally based governmental regimes can be especially difficult.

Moffet and Bregha set out the main types of voluntary regulation (see *Table 4.3*) found in areas such as environmental protection.

These tools attempt such activities as inducing companies to exceed pollution targets by excluding them from other regulations or

Table 4.3 Types of voluntary regulation

1. Legislated compliance plans
2. Regulatory exemption programs
3. Government–industry-negotiated agreements
4. Certification
5. Challenge programmes
6. Design partnerships
7. Standards auditing and accounting

Source: Moffet and Bregha (1999).

enforcement actions, establishing covenants in which companies agree to voluntarily abide by certain standards, establishing labelling provisions or fair trade programmes, providing favourable publicity and treatment for actors exceeding existing standards, promoting cooperation over new innovations and attempting to improve standards attainment by targeted actors through better auditing and evaluation. These are all forms of what Sappington (1994) has termed 'incentive regulation'.

The role played by governments in voluntary regulation is much less explicit than in traditional regulation, but is nevertheless present. Unlike the situation with command and control or delegated regulation, in these instances, governments allow non-governmental actors to regulate themselves without creating specific oversight or monitoring bodies or agencies or empowering legislation. As Gibson (1999: 3) put it:

> By definition voluntary initiatives are not driven by regulatory requirements. They are voluntary in the sense that governments do not have to order them to be undertaken . . . [but] governments play important roles as initiators, signatories, or behind-the-scenes promoters.

While many standards are invoked by government command and control regulation, others can be developed in the private sphere, such as occur in situations where manufacturing companies develop standards for products or where independent certification firms or associations guarantee that certain standards have been met in various kinds of private practices (Gunningham and Rees 1997).

These kinds of self-regulation, however, like certification, are often portrayed as being more 'voluntary' than is actually the case. That is, while non-governmental entities may, in effect, regulate themselves, they typically do so, as Gibson notes, with the implicit or explicit permission of governments, which consciously refrain from regulating activities in a more directly coercive fashion. As long as these private standards are not replaced by government-enforced ones, they represent the acquiescence of a government to the private rules, a form of delegated regulation.

That is, as a 'public' policy instrument, self-regulation still requires some level of state action – 'the shadow of hierarchy' – either in supporting or encouraging development of private self-regulation or retaining the 'iron fist' or the threat of 'real' regulation if private behaviour does not change (Porter and Ronit 2006). This is done in order to ensure that self-regulation meets public objectives and expectations, since any possible savings in administrative costs over more direct forms of legal regulation must be balanced against additional costs to society which might result from ineffective or inefficient administration of voluntary standards, especially those related to non-compliance.

Market creation and maintenance

Paradoxically, as it might seem from its title, another form of indirect regulatory instrument used by government is the use of so-called 'market-based' instruments (Fligstein 1996). These refer to a particular type of regulatory tool in which governments establish property rights frameworks or regimes which then establish various kinds of limits or prices for certain goods and services and allow market actors to work within these 'markets' to allocate goods and services according to price signals (Averch 1990).

Such schemes have often been proposed in many areas, especially in environmental and resource policy, from land and water use and bio-conservation (ecosystem services) to climate change-related emissions control systems, and have also been used in areas such as fisheries and taxi services, in the form of individual transferable quotas (ITQs) or tokens (Townsend et al. 2006). They have also been on prominent display in recent years in order to control greenhouse gas emissions through instruments such as the 'cap and trade' systems created in the European Union and other countries associated with the Kyoto Protocol and climate change mitigation efforts (Heinmiller 2007).

However, despite much publicity, few of these schemes have been implemented given the difficulties of setting prices and limits on items such as pollutants, problems with leakage and poor enforcement in the system and dangers associated with their failure and the inability of governments to bear the blame for problems with these systems, despite their ostensibly arm's-length character (Stavins 1998). Unlike traditional regulation, these designs can have higher costs and be less automatic than expected, and also are very difficult, if not impossible, to target towards specific actors and groups.

Procedural authoritative instruments

Procedural authority-based instruments typically involve the exercise of government authority to recognize or provide preferential treatment or access to certain actors – and hence to fail to recognize others – in the policy process, or to mandate certain procedural requirements in the policy-making process in order to ensure it takes certain views or

perspectives into account. These instruments perform a wide variety
of functions very often in order to gain support or marginalize policy
opponents but also to ensure certain standards and standard practices
are followed in policy choices.

Policy network activation and mobilization tools

In terms of network management activities, many procedural author-
tative tools are involved largely in the 'selective activation' of policy
actors and/or their 'mobilization' through the extension of special recognition in a policy process. The key use of authority is in the extension
of preferential access to decision–makers or regulators for certain views
and actors and not others, or at least to a lesser extent.

These procedural authoritative tools attempt to ensure efficiency
and effectiveness of government actions through activation of policy
actor support. Networks may be structured, for example, through
the creation of various advisory processes, which all rely on the exercise of government authority to recognize and organize specific
sets of policy actors and give them preferential access to government
officials and decision–makers (Pierre 1998). These include advisory
councils, and many of the ad hoc task forces and inquiries, consultations, and public hearings discussed in the previous chapter. These
are oriented towards extending special authoritative status to certain
societal interests or 'stakeholders', that is, those actors with a financial or some other forms of 'stake' in a particular state activity (Hall
and O'Toole 2004).

Phillips and Orsini (2002) list the types of policy process activities
which advisory committees undertake (see *Table 4.4*).

Table 4.4 Actions undertaken by procedural
authoritative instruments

Problem identification
Mobilizing interest
Spanning and bridging activities
Claims-making
Knowledge acquisition
Convening and deliberating
Community capacity-building
Transparency, evaluation and feedback

Source: Phillips and Orsini (2002).

Several distinct types of authoritative network management tools can be identified in this group. Prominent ones include the following.

Sectoral advisory councils

Advisory councils are the best example of procedural authoritative instruments and are very common in market and corporatist governance arrangements. These are more or less permanent bodies established to provide advice to governments – either political-executive or administrative – on an ongoing basis. They are often established on a sectoral (e.g. industry-specific such as an automobile trade advisory committee) basis, but also can be topical (e.g. biomedical ethics) (Brown 1955). These committees play a major role in many areas, but are especially prominent in areas of new technologies where they play a significant role in linking governments to various kinds of expert or 'epistemic' communities (Haas 1992).

The archetypal advisory council is a more or less permanent body used to institutionalize interest group members in government deliberations. They are at least partially if not fully co-optive in nature and intended to align the ideas and actions of the regulated group and the government ministry to which they are attached. However, they can also be more standalone and independent sources of expert advice to governments such as science and technology councils, councils of economic advisors and others (Heinrichs 2005).

Smith (1977) and Brown-John (1979) identify eight main types of advisory committees commonly found in modern liberal-democratic governments. These are shown in *Table 4.5*.

Table 4.5 Types of advisory committees

---

1. General advisory committees – to discuss policy alternatives generated by government, comment on current policies, examine trends and needs and suggest alternatives to status quo.
2. Science and technology advisory committees – to provide expert advice in narrow specialist areas.
3. Special clientele advisory committees – to assist governments to make and implement policies in special sectors of the economy or society.
4. Research advisory committees – lengthy research oriented to tackle large questions.
5. Public conferences – e.g. citizens' assemblies, national forest congresses.
6. Geographic-based advisory committees – to deal with geographic particularities, e.g. in agriculture.
7. Intergovernmental advisory committees – to coordinate between government levels.
8. Interdepartmental committees – to achieve vertical and horizontal coordination in government.

Sources: Smith (1977) and Brown-John (1979).

Brown (1955) lists several purposes of such bodies which stress their network nature (see *Table 4.6*).

Table 4.6 Purposes of advisory boards

1. Source of advice
2. A source of support for regulators
3. A means of popularizing a regulatory regime
4. A 'listening post' for industry and government to listen to each other
5. A means of reaching agreement and resolving conflicts between government and interests
6. An agency for special inquiries
7. A device for patronage
8. A set of ambassadors for an administrative agency

Source: Brown (1955).

These boards are generally very inexpensive and almost invisible. They can be precisely targeted and enhance the automaticity of government. They are also viewed, generally, as non-intrusive. As a result, they have proliferated in all governments in recent years. This proliferation has led in some countries to the passage of legislation to control and standardize the number of advisory committees and their behaviour. The US Advisory Committee Act (1972), for example, specifies membership and guidelines and standard operating procedures for these types of committees (see *Table 4.7*).

Table 4.7 US Advisory Committee Act (1972) criteria

1. Written charter explaining role of committee
2. Timely notice of committee meetings in Federal register
3. Fair and balanced representation on committees
4. Sponsoring agencies prepare minutes of meetings
5. Open committee meetings to the public wherever possible
6. Provide public access to information used by the committee
7. Government given sole authority to convene and adjourn meetings
8. Committees terminated in two years unless renewed or otherwise provided by statute

Source: Smith (1977).

Public consultation, stakeholder and consensus conferences

In addition to more permanent bodies, governments can also organize short-term and long-range mechanisms to provide input and legitimate government policy-making. Increasingly, the role of the public in these processes has been expanded to include participation in the design of the consultation process as well as in making policy recommendations to government. Sometimes mandated by legislation, appropriate levels of government will often elicit public involvement in administrative activities such as regulatory monitoring and environmental impact assessment (Leroux et al. 1998).

Abelson et al. (2003) have noted that these participation efforts can be classified by looking at the procedures, representation and information involved and by looking at their outcomes. Key issues in the design of consultative processes are first who is involved and who is not (for example, whether elites or the public are involved; or whether only stakeholders rather than the public, per se, are consulted) and who makes this determination, for example, government or representative groups.

Many of these efforts are structured as 'stakeholder' representative groups, but 'stakeholder' is a very poorly defined term. Glicken (2000: 306), for example, defines it very broadly as: 'A stakeholder is an individual or group influenced by – and with an ability to significantly impact (either directly or indirectly) – the topical areas of interest'. It is also critical what resources they have, such as access to funding, staff, politicians, information or witnesses, and whether or not their recommendations are binding. Dion lists several of these design criteria on several conjoint continua in *Table 4.8*.

Table 4.8 Types of public consultation – design criteria

1. From the point of view of publicity: how private and secret these consultations are, versus public, open and transparent.
2. From the point of view of official status: whether consultations are unofficial, semi-official or official.
3. From the point of view of origin: whether the consultations are 'organic' (traditional) or 'inorganic' (imposed).
4. From the point of view of imperiousness: whether participation is optional or compulsory.

Source: Dion (1973).

These consultations can cover an extraordinarily wide range of topics – from constitutional issues related to voting systems and the like to much more mundane ones such as city zoning changes. They are typically organized by government agencies, although in some jurisdictions, like Australia, consultants specializing in the organization and delivery of consultation exercises have become much more prominent in recent years (Hendriks and Carson 2008).

Conclusion: regulation – a very flexible instrument

The evolution of regulation as a key policy instrument in the toolbox of modern government is a well-known story. From the development of the principle of delegated legislation in the early years of the evolution of the modern state to the first creation of specialized quasi-judicial independent regulatory commissions in the United States after the Civil War, the gradual development of bureaucratic expertise and capacity in the social and economic realms is a defining characteristic of the legal and corporatist modes of governance found in many policy sectors and regulations and regulatory agencies are a central feature in many policy designs (Scherer 2008).

Debates about the merits of this development continues in many areas, however, especially those sectors which could be organized along market lines. For example, a large literature exists on whether or not regulations serve the public or the private interest (Stigler 1975) and whether or not they contribute to economic efficiency by correcting market failures or instead create new government ones (Wolf 1987). The discussion has generated a plethora of studies about the merits of particular types of regulation over others, the problems of regulatory capture and other concerns related to the difficulties of legislative and judicial oversight of regulatory activities (Gilardi 2002).

The early 1980s was a turning point in this debate on regulation in many countries, as the idea that regulations were conceived and executed solely in the public interest came under heavy attack from a wide range of critics. Governments led by right-wing politicians in many countries, like Ronald Reagan in the USA and Margaret Thatcher in the UK, but also Labour governments in New Zealand and elsewhere, further fanned popular sentiment against regulations and put deregulation and the search for alternatives to traditional 'command and control' regulation at the centre of policy reform agendas designed to address declines in productivity, persistent inflation and high unemployment present at the time (Howlett and Ramesh 2006). Many governments began at this time to experiment with alternate forms of regulation, especially 'voluntary regulation'.

Many 'deregulation' measures, however, are commonsense reforms intended to iron out shortcomings, anomalies and obsolescence in existing regulations rather than a response to any particular systemic pressure. The nature and extent of problems change, as do solutions available to deal with them and in many cases regulatory regimes and regulations have been reformed rather than rescinded. It must also be noted that at the same time that some deregulation has occurred, re-regulation of many sectors has also taken place. And, as the discussion in this chapter has shown, an explosion of the use of procedural authoritative implementation tools has also occurred over this same time period.

References

Abelson, Julia, Pierre-Gerlier Forest, John Eyles, Patricia Smith, Elisabeth Martin, and Francois-Pierre Gauvin. "Deliberations about Deliberative Methods: Issues in the Design and Evaluation of Public Participation Processes." *Social Science and Medicine* 57 (2003): 239–51.

Ajzen, Icek. "The Theory of Planned Behavior." *Organizational Behavior and Human Decision Processes* 50, no. 2 (1991): 179–211.

Averch, Harvey. *Private Markets and Public Interventions: A Primer for Policy Designers.* Pittsburgh, PA: University of Pittsburgh Press, 1990.

Baldwin, Robert, and Martin Cave. *Understanding Regulation: Theory, Strategy and Practice.* Oxford: Oxford University Press, 1999.

Brockman, Joan. "'Fortunate Enough to Obtain and Keep the Title of Profession'; Self-Regulating Organizations and the Enforcement of Professional Monopolies." *Canadian Public Administration* 41, no. 4 (1998): 587–621.

Brown, David S. "The Public Advisory Board as an Instrument of Government." *Public Administration Review* 15 (1955): 196–201.

Brown-John, C. Lloyd. "Advisory Agencies in Canada: An Introduction." *Canadian Public Administration* 22, no. 1 (1979): 72–91.

Cushman, Robert Eugene. *The Independent Regulatory Commissions.* London: Oxford University Press, 1941.

Dion, Leon. 'The Politics of Consultation.' *Government and Opposition* 8, no. 3 (1973): 332–53.

Dyerson, Romano, and Frank Mueller. "Intervention by Outsiders: A Strategic Perspective on Government Industrial Policy." *Journal of Public Policy* 13, no. 1 (1993): 69–88.

Edley, Christopher F. J. *Administrative Law: Rethinking Judicial Control of Bureaucracy.* New Haven, CT: Yale University Press, 1990.

Elgie, Robert. "Why Do Governments Delegate Authority to Quasi-Autonomous Agencies? The Case of Independent Administrative Authorities in France." *Governance* 19, no. 2 (2006): 207–27.

Fligstein, Neil. "Markets and Politics: A Political-Cultural Approach to Market Institutions." *American Sociological Review* 61, (August 1996): 656–73.

Gibson, Robert B. *Voluntary Initiatives: The New Politics of Corporate Greening.* Peterborough, ON: Broadview Press, 1999.

Gilardi, Fabrizio. "Policy Credibility and Delegation to Independent Regulatory Agencies: A Comparative Empirical Analysis." *Journal of European Public Policy* 9, no. 6 (2002): 873–93.

Glicken, Jessica. "Getting Stakeholder Participation 'Right': A Discussion of Participatory Processes and Possible Pitfalls." *Environmental Science and Policy* 3 (2000): 305–10.

Gunningham, Neil, and Joseph Rees. "Industry Self-Regulation: An Institutional Perspective." *Law Policy* 19, no. 4 (1997): 363–414.

Haas, Peter M. "Introduction: Epistemic Communities and International Policy Coordination." *International Organization* 46, no. 1 (1992): 1–36.

Hall, Thad E., and Laurence J. O'Toole. "Shaping Formal Networks through the Regulatory Process." *Administration & Society* 36, no. 2 (2004): 186–207.

Heinmiller, B. Timothy. "The Poltiics of 'Cap and Trade' Policies." *Natural Resources Journal* 47, no. 2 (2007): 445–67.

Heinrichs, Harald. "Advisory Systems in Pluralistic Knowledge Societies: A Criteria-Based Typology to Assess and Optimize Environmental Policy Advice." In *Democratization of Expertise?* edited by Sabine Maasen and Peter Weingart, 24, 41–61. Berlin and Heidelberg: Springer-Verlag, 2005.

Hendriks, Carolyn, and Lyn Carson. "Can the Market Help the Forum? Negotiating the Commercialization of Deliberative Democracy." *Policy Sciences* 41, no. 4 (December 1, 2008): 293–313.

Heritier, Adrienne, and Drik Lehmkuhl. "Introduction: The Shadow of Hierarchy and New Modes of Governance." *Journal of Public Policy* 28, no. 1 (2008): 1–17.

Jacobzone, Stephane. "Independent Regulatory Authorities in OECD Countries: An Overview." In *Designing Independent and Accountable Regulatory Authorities for High Quality Regulation – Proceedings of an Expert Meeting in London, United Kingdom 10–11 January 2005*, edited by OECD Working Party on Regulatory Management and Reform, 72–100. Paris: OECD, 2005.

Jordana, Jacint, and David Levi-Faur, eds. *The Politics of Regulation: Institutions and Regulatory Reforms for the Age of Governance.* Cheltenham: Edward Elgar Jordana, J, 2004.

Kerwin, Cornelius M. *Rulemaking: How Government Agencies Write Law and Make Policy.* Washington, DC: CQ Press, 1999.

Keyes, John Mark. "Power Tools: The Form and Function of Legal Instruments for Government Action." *Canadian Journal of Administrative Law and Practice* 10 (1996): 133–74.

Kiviniemi, Markku. "Public Policies and Their Targets: A Typology of the Concept of Implementation." *International Social Science Journal* 38, no. 108 (1986): 251–66.

Kuhlmann, Ellen, and Judith Allsop. "Professional Self-Regulation in a Changing Architecture of Governance: Comparing Health Policy in the UK and Germany." *Policy & Politics* 36, no. 2 (2008): 173–89.

Leroux, Thérèse, Marie Hirtle, and Louis-Nicolas Fortin. "An Overview of Public Consultation Mechanisms Developed to Address the Ethical and Social Issues Raised by Biotechnology." *Journal of Consumer Policy* 21, no. 4 (December 1, 1998): 445–81.

May, Peter J. "Social Regulation." In *The Tools of Government: A Guide to the New Governance,* edited by Lester M. Salamon, 156–85. New York: Oxford University Press, 2002.

McCubbins, Mathew D., and Thomas Schwartz. "Congressional Oversight Overlooked: Police Patrols Versus Fire Alarms." *American Journal of Political Science* 28, no. 1 (1984): 165–79.

Mitnick, Barry M. "The Concept of Regulation." *Bulletin of Business Research* 53, no. 5 (1978): 1–20.

Moffet, John, and François Bregha. 1999. "Non-Regulatory Environmental Measures." In *Voluntary Initiatives: The New Politics of Corporate Greening*, edited by R. B. Gibson, 15–31. Peterborough: Broadview Press.

Phillips, Susan D., and Michael Orsini. 2002. *Mapping the Links: Citizen Involvement in Policy Processes.* Ottawa, ON: Canadian Policy Research Networks.

Pierre, Jon. "Public Consultation and Citizen Participation: Dilemmas of Policy Advice." In *Taking Stock: Assessing Public Sector Reforms*, edited by B. Guy Peters and Donald J. Savoie, 137–63. Montreal, QC: McGill-Queen's Press, 1998.

Porter, Tony, and Karsten Ronit. "Self-Regulation as Policy Process: The Multiple and Crisscrossing Stages of Private Rule-Making." *Policy Sciences* 39 (2006): 41–72.

Ramesh, M., and Michael Howlett. *Deregulation and Its Discontents: Rewriting the Rules in Asia.* Aldershot: Edward Elgar, 2006.

Reagan, Michael D. *Regulation: The Politics of Policy.* Boston, MA: Little Brown, 1987.

Rosenbloom, David H. "Administrative Law and Regulation." In *Handbook of Public Administration*, edited by Jack Rabin, W. Bartley Hildreth, and Gerald J. Miller, 635–96. London: CRC Press, 2007.

Royer, Annie. "The Emergence of Agricultural Marketing Boards Revisited: A Case Study in Canada." *Canadian Journal of Agricultural Economics* 56 (2008): 509–22.

Sappington, David E. M. "Designing Incentive Regulation." *Review of Industrial Organization* 9, no. 3 (June 1, 1994): 245–72.

Scherer, Frederic M. *The Historical Foundations of Communications Regulation.* Boston, MA: Harvard University, 2008.

Scott, Colin. "Analysing Regulatory Space: Fragmented Resources and Institutional Design." *Public Law* (Summer 2001): 329–53.

Smith, Thomas B. "Advisory Committees in the Public Policy Process." *International Review of Administrative Sciences* 43, no. 2 (1977): 153–66.

Stavins, Robert N. "What Can We Learn from the Grand Policy Experiment? Lessons from SO2 Allowance Trading." *Journal of Economic Perspectives* 12, no. 3 (1998): 69–88.

Stigler, George Joseph. *The Citizen and the State: Essays on Regulation.* Chicago, IL: University of Chicago Press, 1975.

Tallontire, Anna. "CSR and Regulation: Towards a Framework for Understanding Private Standards Initiatives in the Agri-Food Chain." *Third World Quarterly* 28, no. 4 (2007): 775–91.

Townsend, Ralph E., James McColl, and Michael D. Young. "Design Principles for Individual Transferable Quotas." *Marine Policy* 30 (2006): 131–41.

Tuohy, Carolyn J., and Alan D. Wolfson. "Self-Regulation: Who Qualifies?" In *The Professions and Public Policy*, edited by Phillip Slayton and Michael J. Trebilcock, 111–22. Toronto, ON: University of Toronto Press, 1978.

Weimer, David L. "Public and Private Regulation of Organ Transplantation: Liver Allocation and the Final Rule." *Journal of Health Politics, Policy and Law* 32, no. 1 (February 2007): 9–49.

Wolf Jr, Charles. "Markets and Non-Market Failures: Comparison and Assessment." *Journal of Public Policy* 7, no. 1 (1987): 43–70.

Wonka, Arndt, and Berthold Rittberger. "Credibility, Complexity and Uncertainty: Explaining the Institutional Independence of 29 EU – Agencies." *West European Politics* 33, no. 4 (2010): 730.

Wu, Irene. "Who Regulates Phones, Television, and the Internet? What Makes a Communications Regulator Independent and Why It Matters." *Perspectives on Politics* 6, no. 4 (2008): 769–83.

Ziller, Jacques. "Public Law: A Tool for Modern Management, Not an Impediment to Reform." *International Review of Administrative Sciences* 71, no. 2 (2005): 267–77.

5 Financial implementation tools

Financial substantive tools are not synonymous with all government spending, since much of this goes to fund direct service delivery and also support regulatory agencies (as well as to provide information, which will be discussed in Chapter 6). Rather, such tools are specific techniques of governance involved in transferring treasure resources to or from actors in order to encourage them to undertake some activity desired by governments through the provision of financial incentives, or to discourage them through the imposition of financial costs.

Like organizational and authoritative tools, there are many different permutations of these instruments and mechanisms. In fact, they can be calibrated down to the decimal point, since they involve the transfer of money, or goods and services with a calculable dollar value, between governments and between governments and non-governmental actors and organizations. And, as such, their exact configuration is virtually infinite in variety. Nevertheless, like organizational and authority-based tools, their basic types are few and categorizable according to what kind of treasure resource they rely upon to extract expected behaviour from targeted organizations, groups and individuals. Transfers can be either in cash or tax-based, but also can be made through a wide range of 'cash equivalents', for example, procurement, loans guarantees, insurance or vouchers, amongst others. Both principal types and some of the many alternate means are discussed in the chapter.

Substantive financial instruments

The use of treasure resources in policy designs to allow states to obtain their substantive goals is very common and is compatible with most modes of governance, especially market-based ones.

Modern liberal democratic states spend billions annually on many different programmes ranging from healthcare to retirement savings involving the use of these tools. However, in some areas, such as industrial activity, some efforts have been made in recent years – for example, through provisions of free-trade treaties and the like which ban subsidies to businesses and lower or eliminate import duties– to restrict their use. These efforts have been only partially successful, though, often resulting in the transformation of cash-based incentives and disincentives to other forms of financial tools, rather than their complete abandonment.

Cash–based financial tools

Grants, subsidies and user fees

Haider defines grants as 'payments in cash or in kind (or charges) to lower units of government, non-profits or profit-seeking companies, NGOs (and individuals) to support public purposes' (Haider 1989: 94). All substantive grants are subsidies or 'unearned savings to offset production costs' and are one of the oldest forms of financial tool through which governments pay companies, organizations or individuals to do (or not to do – like agricultural subsidies for not growing corn or wheat, etc.) some (un)desired form of activity (Lybecker and Freeman 2007).

This is the 'carrot' in instrument and implementation models based on the idea of the use of 'carrots and sticks' (sticks being regulations or penalties by governments in their efforts to influence non-governmental actors) (Balch 1980). Many, many such schemes exist, from the use of Feed-in-Tariffs to promote the use of renewable energy supplies such as solar panels and wind power, to the payment of cash to parents to send their children to school in various kinds of 'Conditional Cash Transfers' or CCTs found in countries from the Philippines to Brazil and Ghana.

User fees are the most straightforward financial disincentive (one of the 'sticks' available to governments), as they, too, simply attempt to affect target behaviour by increasing the cost of doing some action. While straightforward in principle, however, in practice, their design can be quite complex depending on exactly what it is that a government wishes to accomplish through their imposition, for example, revenue generation, goods or service rationing or some combination of the two, and, as pointed out in Chapter 2, how non-governmental actors are likely to react to such charges (Deber et al. 2008).

These kinds of cash-based tools use the direct transfer of treasure or fiscal resources from governments to some other actor or vice versa in the form of monetary payments. They vary along several dimensions. They can, to cite only a few examples, be large or small, a single instance or multi-year in nature, tax deductible (which increases their size) or not, used alone or in combination with other instruments (for instance, in conjunction with the use of public enterprises in regional development programmes or regulation in the effort to modernize factories to control emissions), matched or not by recipients or linked to some other item (e.g. a per capita grant) (Leeuw 1998). They typically can be very precisely targeted down to the level of the individual and the individual firm or plant, and can be very precisely calibrated. They are also quite visible as they appear in public accounts and are considered to be more intrusive than information-based tools, but less so than authority- or organization-based ones. They can also be designed in such a way as to enhance their automaticity, although this is more the case with tax- and royalty-based payments, as discussed in the following section.

Tax- or royalty-based financial instruments

The second main type of substantive treasure-based implementation instrument involves those which are based not on direct cash transfers, but rather on indirect transfers mediated through the tax system, or, in some countries, through the use of royalty systems designed to capture natural resource rents. These tools are much less visible and often do not require extensive budgetary approval since they involve not collecting revenues rather than gathering them which often requires explicit legislative approval. In these systems, a government can forego tax or royalty income they would otherwise have collected from an individual, organization or firm, which serves like a subsidy, providing an incentive to targets to undertake the activity by delivering favourable tax treatment, or, in the case of tools which increase taxes on certain kinds of activity, to not undertake that activity or to undertake less of it (Surrey 1970).

Tax- and royalty-based expenditures

Tax expenditures or 'tax incentives' come in many kinds. Maslove defines them as 'special provisions in the tax law providing for preferred treatment and consequently resulting in revenue losses (or gains)' (Maslove 1979). These can be 'paid in advance' and can be carried forward for numbers of years, and, like cash-based schemes, can be 'matched' by other sources of funds, range in size and significance, and can be used in conjunction with other instruments.

Different subtypes exist depending on 'where' government tax revenue is forgone. *Tax incentives* generally involve deductions from corporate or personal income, meaning their actual effect on a target group is determined by the marginal rate of taxation individual persons or firms must pay. Their effect therefore varies from group to group and activity to activity. *Tax credits*, on the other hand, are direct deductions from taxes owed, not taxable income, and therefore their size is the same regardless of the tax rates individual taxpayers face. Tax credits are typically the only ones which can be 'negative', in the sense that they can be used to push a taxpayer's tax load beyond zero so that a refund (or real cash transfer) may ensue. However, most tax expenditures will only push a taxpayer's taxes to zero, meaning their effect also remains conditional on the amount of taxes targets pay (Woodside 1979).

These same kinds of schemes can also be developed with transfers from non-tax-based revenue such as resource royalty payments or other forms of economic rents. Governments can, for example, promote oil and gas exploration by allowing energy companies to write off some portion of their exploration costs against royalties they would otherwise have to pay when they develop a well.

Excise taxes

Excise taxes are another treasure-based tool, one that acts as a disincentive to individuals, organizations and groups to undertake specific actions and activities. Cnossen (2005: 2) defines these as 'all selective taxes and related levies and charges on goods and services'. They have several general purposes: (1) to raise revenue for general purposes, (2) to offset 'external costs' associated with the activity, like the costs of dealing with negative health outcomes from smoking, (3) to discourage consumption and (4) to pay for public goods like roads and infrastructure from freight and shipping taxes and charges.

Raising revenue through taxes is, of course, the oldest technique of government practised, from taxes placed on road use by the Romans to the tea tax US colonists rebelled against at the Boston Tea Party and is exercised by every level of government, from the local to the national (Nowlan 1994). Using taxes to offset costs of production – to pay for pollution clean-up or health consequences of tobacco use in order to correct production or consumption 'externalities' like pollution or carbon emissions which otherwise would be passed onto the general public – is a much newer form (Pope and Owen 2009). A similar effort involves the so-called 'vice taxes' collected in recent years for activities such as gambling, alcohol consumption, lotteries or, more frequently in the present era, various forms of 'virtuous' 'green' taxes such as those designed to cover the cost of recycling car batteries or used oil or paint, returnable bottle deposits or even carbon emissions, all designed to offset the costs of the activities to external actors and society (Cnossen 2005). The use of motor fuel taxes to cover the cost of road construction or mass transit is an example of using specialized taxes to pay for public goods.

Such taxes generally discourage the taxed activity by raising its price. This, of course, can be a mixed blessing for activities such as public transit, and can often result in unintended consequences for items taxed in order to raise revenues, both in terms of taxpayer resistance and upset, and in the unintended encouragement of the increased use of non-taxed items or substitute goods and services. They are generally inexpensive to establish, although they require an extensive revenue collection and enforcement presence to avoid evasion, and can be either highly visible, if added onto prices, or almost invisible, if included with posted prices. They can be targeted to specific kinds of goods and services and set up to be highly automated. They are generally considered to be quite intrusive by those paying them, however, which is the main reason they are often excluded from policy designs (Hofmann et al. 2014).

Cash or tax-equivalent financial tools

Both cash and tax or royalty-based transfers are relatively straightforward examples of tools which provide financial incentives and disincentives to policy actors to undertake or refrain from undertaking specific activities encouraged or discouraged by governments. However, such encouragement and discouragement do not always require a direct or indirect cash transfer. Governments are also able to provide financial incentives through the much less direct use of their spending powers to offset costs or provide additional benefits to policy targets. Several of the more prominent of these tools are discussed in the following section.

Preferential procurement

Preferential procurement involves the use of government purchases to subsidize companies or investors which agree to abide by specific provisions of government contracts. These can extend to preferential treatment for firms which, for example, employ the disabled or women, or ethnic or linguistic minorities, but also often extend to special favourable treatment for small business, national defence contractors and regional development schemes in which investors receive government contracts if they agree to locate factories or distribution or other services in specially designated regions (Rolfstam 2009).

Procurement schemes play a major part in efforts by governments to promote the 'third sector' or volunteer community- or group-based delivery of public services discussed in Chapters 3 and 4 and are often a part of corporatist governance arrangements (Dollery and Wallis 2003). In many cases, it may be illegal or unconstitutional for a government to directly deliver funding to such groups, especially if NGOs have a religious or 'faith base' which can violate constitutional and other legal limits separating church and state activities (Black et al. 2004). However, these groups may still be able to receive favourable treatment such as in bidding for government contracts, often making procurement an important part of their funding base and a *de facto* subsidy to their other religious activities (Carmel and Harlock 2008).

Like direct cash subsidies, many trade agreements attempt to ban procurement plans which favour national over international suppliers, but these provisions do not extend to favourable treatment for marginalized groups or individuals or companies linked to national defence and security. Such procurement schemes, of course, by extending favourable treatment to some contractors, also act as a disincentive to non-favoured groups and firms which are discouraged from bidding for contracts and other services to the extent of the subsidy provided (McCrudden 2004). The main advantage of such forms of subsidy over other forms of payments is their low visibility profile, which encourages their use. They can be organized in many different ways, from open-bidding to closed, and involve a variety of clauses and requisites concerning qualification for them (Bajari and Tadelis 2001).

Favourable insurance and loan guarantees

Insurance or loan guarantees also act as a subsidy to the extent that government backing helps to secure loans, thereby raising the reliability of borrowers, altering the types of borrowers who might otherwise fail to qualify for loans or reducing interest payments and charges that individuals and companies would otherwise have to pay (Maslove 1983). Any difference in cost constitutes a subsidy to the party involved.

Such guarantees are very common in areas such as student loans and housing, for example, in which governments agree to serve as the guarantor of loans to banks which otherwise would reject most students and applicants as too risky. They are also common in areas such as technological innovation and export development, whereby a government may provide insurance to a domestic firm to help it offset the risk of undertaking some product development activity, or provide a foreign company or government with assurance that a contract will be fulfilled by the supplying firm.

Some loans can also be made directly to individuals and firms on a 'conditionally repayable' basis; that is, whereby a loan turns into a grant if the conditions are successfully met, for example, in constructing a factory and operating it for a set period of time. These tools are almost invisible, can be precisely targeted and are often considered to be less intrusive than grants and direct cash or tax transfers, making them a popular choice for policy designs in sectors which governments want to encourage.

Vouchers for public services

Vouchers are 'money replacements' provided by governments to certain groups in order to allow them to purchase specified goods and services in specific amounts. These are typically used when a government does not trust someone to use a cash transfer for its intended purpose, for example, with vouchers for food (food stamps), child care or welfare hotel/housing payments.

Some governments like Denmark and Sweden, however, also use these to provide some freedom of choice for consumers to select particular kinds of public services (usually education) in order to promote competition within monopoly provision systems or to allow equitable funding arrangements between providers based on specific attributes – such as schools provided by different religious denominations (Klitgaard 2008). These can lead to grey markets (when food stamps, for example, are sold at a discount to 'undeserving' recipients) and may not improve service delivery if there is little choice provided in the supply of goods and services for which vouchers are issued (Valkama and Bailey 2001). As a result, although often mooted, vouchers appear only rarely in policy designs.

Sales of state assets at below-market prices

Governments can also sell off or 'rent out' certain items – from the TV and radio spectrum to old or surplus equipment, buildings and land and resources (Sunnevag 2000). If prices are set below market rates, then this is a subsidy to investors and businesses. Many privatizations of formerly state-owned firms in collapsed socialist countries in the 1990s, for example, involved this kind of sale, including for lucrative mineral and oil and gas rights, which made billions of dollars for the many former officials who were favoured in these deals. Given the costs involved, and their generally high profile, however, this tool also does not feature very often in policy designs in countries which are stable and solvent.

Procedural financial instruments

Treasure resources, of course, like organizational and authoritative ones, can also be used to alter the nature of policy processes. Procedural financial tools are generally used to attempt to alter or control aspects of the interest articulation and aggregation systems in contemporary states by creating or encouraging the formation of associations and groups where this activity might not otherwise occur, or, more prosaically, by rewarding government friends and punishing enemies through various kinds of payment schemes or penalties.

Phillip Schmitter, in his comparative studies of European systems, argued that the interest articulation systems in different countries form a spectrum, ranging from 'free market', 'competitive' pluralism to 'state-sponsored oligarchic corporatism' (see Figure 5.1). In Schmitter's (1977) view, pluralism is a system of interest articulation in which interest groups are 'free-forming', have voluntary membership and are multiple and non-monopolistic/competitive. That is, more than one group can represent individual members.

Corporatist regimes are the opposite – they require state licencing, have compulsory membership and are monopolistic. Corporatism was the official mode of social organization in pre-World War II fascist countries, however, and in order to avoid this association and connotation, modern studies tend to use the term 'neocorporatism' to distinguish modern forms of (liberal-democratic) corporatism found in states such as Austria or Sweden, from older ones – though examples also exist of this form in liberal-democratic states in crises, such as during wartime or during the Rooseveltian New Deal in the United States. Other variants also exist, for example, consociationalism – where corporatist systems exist but divisions are on ethnic or religious grounds (Atkinson and Coleman 1992). Until recently, interest mobilization and representation in North America was thought to be largely pluralist whereby it was argued that interest group formation was a quasi-automatic, 'naturalistic process' in which state activity was minimal. The empirical basis for this assessment, however, was lacking (Walker 1991).

Pluralism ———— Neo-pluralism ———— Societal Corporatism ———— State Corporatism

(Freely associational) ————————————————→ (State sanctioned)

Figure 5.1 Spectrum of interest articulation systems.
Source: Schmitter (1977).

Olson's (1965) view of the 'collective action problems' interest groups face in these different governance contexts is an important insight helpful to understanding the rationales for the government use of procedural financial instrument in these situations. Olson argued that in any political system, some individuals have fewer incentives and more disincentives to form and join interest groups than others – for example, someone benefitting from some proposed government action might have a stronger motivation to lobby for it, than would someone who stood neither to gain nor suffer from it. As a result, in a 'free association' system, there would be a tendency for specific affected interests – for example, businesses negatively affected by regulation – to form groups and pressure governments, while other more general interests – for example, to retain tough environmental standards on industry – would be poorly represented. Due to this unequal distribution of the costs and benefits of political action in many issue areas in pluralist systems, 'general interest' groups are thought to be unlikely to form, or if they did, would be quickly captured by 'special interests' who had more to gain from their existence and activities (Strolovitch 2006).

Governments, however, can play a major, though little studied, role even in pluralist countries in affecting this general pattern of interest group behaviour by either encouraging or discouraging interest group formation and activity (Toke 2000). These activities are little publicized, but quite common. Governments can do this, for example, by creating (or not) systems of associational rights which allow groups to form, using their actions and resources to publicize events and issues, and providing funds for the creation and maintenance of groups. Procedural financial implementation tools are key ones used to affect these kinds of interest group system behaviour.

These tools generally fall into two types, those which are used to create or help support the formation of interest groups and those which help to activate or mobilize them. The former can be thought as 'network creation tools', while the latter can be considered as 'network mobilization tools'.

Financial policy network creation tools

Although their activities in this domain are often hidden from view, governments are very often actively involved in the creation and organization of policy networks. An important activity is the use of government financial resources either to create the organizations which go into the establishment of a policy network – research institutes, think tanks, government departments and the like – or to facilitate the interaction of already existing but separate units into a more coherent network structure (Hudson et al. 2007).

Funding is very often provided to think tanks and other policy research units and brokers by governments, either in the form of direct funding or as contracts (Rich 2004). More controversial, however, and at the same time not very well understood, is the role governments play in funding interest groups (Anheier et al. 1997).

Interest group creation

Provision of seed money is a key factor in interest group creation (Nownes 2004). King (1991), for example, found that the percentage of groups that received aid from outside groups in startups in the United States was 34 per cent for profit sector groups, 60 per cent for non-profit and 89 per cent for citizens' groups. Nownes and Neeley (1996) surveyed 121 national public interest groups in the USA in the mid-1990s, and uncovered a pattern of extensive foundation support in terms of how their origin was financed (*Table 5.1*). While this survey revealed little direct government involvement, it did show that foundations provided a large percentage of the funding for pressure group creation, and since these operate under special tax treatment in the USA, this gives the US federal government a substantial indirect role in interest group creation in that country (Lowry 1999).

Table 5.1 Average percentage of 'seed money' obtained by groups from each source by group type

Source	Type of group (%)				
	Patronage	Societal disturbance	Personal disturbance	Splinter	Generic entrepreneurial
Foundations	38	38	0	23	19
The government	0	0	0	0	0
Corporations	0	1	17	3	2
Other					
Associations	32	11	3	0	2
Individuals	19	18	3	28	29
Personal funds	0	31	60	43	43
Other[a]	11	1	17	3	5
Total	100	100	100	100	100
n	10	12	6	16	16

Source: Nownes and Neeley (1996).
[a] Includes loans, merchandise sales, fees for service and special events.

In other countries however, a much more direct role is played by governments, sometimes also accompanied by a substantial indirect role through foundations, but sometimes not. In Canada, for example, Pal (1993) noted that many of the prominent national interest groups in specific sectors, such as the Canadian Day Care Advocacy Association, the Canadian Congress for Learning Opportunities among Women and the Canadian Ethnocultural Council, emerged from conferences and workshops organized by federal government departments in the 1980s and the 1990s and benefited from favorable treatment of donations as charitable or otherwise tax deductible expenses. Similar results can be found in many other jurisdictions. This activity is generally low profile and inexpensive, but can be considered intrusive and is not all that easily targeted, making it a less popular instrument in policy designs than network mobilization (see below). However, where interest groups do not exist, governments may have little choice but to facilitate their creation if they wish to ensure representation of these interests and viewpoints.

Financial network mobilization tools

A second key type of activity undertaken by governments through the use of procedural financial policy tools relates less to the creation of new groups and networks than to the reorientation of older, already existing ones. Again, in the case of think tanks and other such actors, this can be accomplished through various forms of government contracting and procurement, notably consulting and commissioning (discussed in Chapter 3 above) (Howlett and Migone 2013). A significant target for this kind of funding is interest groups.

Interest group alteration/manipulation/co-optation

Cash funds or the tax system are used in many countries to alter interest group behaviour. The aim may be simply to neutralize or co-opt a vocal opponent of government (Kash 2008), but can also be a more broad-based effort to 'even out the playing field' for groups which lack the kinds of resources available to other groups (such as business) to mobilize and pressure governments to adopt policies of which they approve (Furlong and Kerwin 2004).

Most business groups, as well as many others, prefer 'insider action' and only revert to 'outside agitation' in order to attract new members in a competitive situation with other groups (Binderkrantz 2005). Designing these programmes can therefore be quite complex (Phillips and Hebb 2010). Governments often use this tool to counterbalance, for example, extensive lobbying on the part of business interests.

This has been going on for some time although in the overall scheme of things it is relatively new. In the USA, for example, Lowry (1999) found that two main types of foundations exist – company-sponsored and independent – and both take active roles not only in interest group creation (discussed above) but also in funding interest group activities on a one-off or continual basis. In the United States, in 1992, for example, he uncovered 463 grants made by 37 company founda-tions and 125 independent foundations just to environmental groups, $32.6 million from independent foundations versus only $1.5 million from company-sponsored foundations. Again, given the favourable tax treatment foundations enjoy in the USA, this gives the US govern-ment a substantial indirect role in interest group activity as well as their creation.

In other countries, as with interest group creation, foundations are less important, and governments instead provide 'sustaining' funding after groups are created. Stanbury (1993), for example, examined the Canadian federal public accounts as early as 1986–87, and found 17 federal departments gave $185 million to over 500 groups (excluding non-policy groups like those providing shelters for battered women). Over 50 organizations in Stanbury's sample were funded by a single federal agency – the Federal Secretary of State – mainly in the area of multiculturalism.

Similarly, Pal found a total of $80 million going from the Federal Sec-retary of State to minority language groups over the period 1970–82, $50 million in 1978–82 alone, while multicultural groups received over $125 million from 1976 to 1988 and $94 million in 1983 to 1988. Women's programmes received $63 from 1973 to 1988 and $46 million over 1984 to 1988 (Stasiulis 1988). Phillips (1991) found the Federal Secretary of State to have spent $130 million over much the same period on over 3,000 groups, with five major areas accounting for about one-third of all recipients: 337 groups for official languages, 457 women's groups, 195 disabled groups, 160 aboriginal groups and 175 multicultural groups.

One hundred and sixty of these groups were defined only as 'public interest groups' (or classical pressure groups) and received $24 million from federal departments alone that year. Burt (1990) similarly surveyed the sources of funding received by 144 women's groups (24 per cent of the estimated 686 such groups in Canada at the time) in the early 1980s, and found the government was the single largest donor by far for most types of groups, far outstripping membership dues (see *Table 5.2*).

Table 5.2 Source of funding for women's groups (Canada)

Most important source of funds	Type of group (%)			
	Traditional	Status of women	Service	Shelter
Government	33	40	38	52
Dues	8	20	9	0
Fund-raising	17	7	2	11
Other n/a	42	33	51	37
	100	100	100	100

Source: Burt (1990).

Similarly, in Europe, Mahoney and Beckstrand (2009) identified 1,164 civil society groups that received funding from the European Commission in 2003–7. They shared in 120 million euros of funding at the EU level and another 75 million in international-, national- and subnational-level funding. These were primarily groups operating at the EU level in areas such as youth, sports, education and cultural activities in support of the EC mandate to develop a supra-national EU identity and civil society.

This kind of funding is almost invisible, can be precisely targeted and, although often considered intrusive, is quite common. As such it is a growing area and a prominent feature of many contemporary policy designs.

Conclusion: treasure – an effective but depletable resource

The use of financial resources is one of the oldest forms of government activity and instrument use. The use of substantive treasure-based implementation instruments is quite common in many policy designs, and in terms of size and impact, almost is as significant as direct government service delivery or regulation.

The use of this resource, as Hood (1986) noted, however, is sometimes restricted by a lack of treasure resources, either because a country is poor and simply cannot generate revenue or, as has happened in jurisdictions like California, for example, because of various measures which prevent or limit government access to substantial taxpayer wealth. However, notwithstanding these limitations, in general, all governments spend considerable sums encouraging certain activities and discouraging others through the use of various kinds of fiscal and monetary tools and techniques. An important trend in this area, noted by Howard (1997), is towards the increased use of tax-based incentives rather than subsidies. This is due to a number of reasons, including the anti-subsidy trade treaties cited above, but often reflects concerns with and preferences for (in)visibility and automaticity in designs.

As for procedural financial tool uses, as mentioned earlier, the use of these techniques is also increasing at a substantial rate. Although the exact mechanisms used vary from country to country, such as the use of indirect foundations in the USA, compared to more direct government allocations in many other jurisdictions, these tools are an understudied and little-examined, but nonetheless critical, component of many policy designs.

References

Anheier, Helmut K., Stefan Toepler, and S. Wojciech Sokolowski. "The Implications of Government Funding for Non-Profit Organizations: Three Propositions." *International Journal of Public Sector Management* 10, no. 3 (1997): 190–213.

Atkinson, Michael M., and William D. Coleman. "Policy Networks, Policy Communities and the Problems of Governance." *Governance* 5, no. 2 (1992): 154–80.

Bajari, Patrick, and Steven Tadelis. "Incentives versus Transaction Costs: A Theory of Procurement Contracts." *RAND Journal of Economics* 32, no. 3 (2001): 387–407.

Balch, George I. "The Stick, the Carrot, and Other Strategies: A Theoretical Analysis of Governmental Intervention." *Law and Policy Quarterly* 2, no. 1 (1980): 35–60.

Binderkrantz, Anne. "Interest Group Strategies: Navigating Between Privileged Access and Strategies of Pressure." *Political Studies* 53 (2005): 694–715.

Black, Amy E., Douglas L. Koopman, and David K. Ryden. *Of Little Faith: The Politics of George W. PBush's Faith-Based Initiative.* Washington, DC: Georgetyown University Press, 2004.

Burt, Sandra. "Canadian Women's Groups in the 1980s: Organizational Development and Policy Influence." *Canadian Public Policy* 16, no. 1 (1990): 17–28.

Carmel, Emma, and Jenny Harlock. "Instituting the 'Third Sector' as a Governable Terrain: Partnership, Procurement and Performance in the UK." *Policy & Politics* 36, no. 2 (2007): 155–71.

Cnossen, Sijbren. *Theory and Practice of Excise Taxation: Smoking, Drinking, Gambling, Polluting and Driving.* Oxford: Oxford University Press, 2005.

Deber, Raisa, Marcus J. Hollander, and Philip Jacobs. "Models of Funding and Reimbursment in Health Care: A Conceptual Framework." *Canadian Public Administration* 51, no. 3 (2008): 381–405.

Dollery, Brain E., and Joe L. Wallis. *The Political Economy of the Voluntary Sector: A Reappraisal of the Comparative Institutional Advantage of Voluntary Organizations.* Cheltenham: Edward Elgar, 2003.

Furlong, Scott R., and Cornelius M. Kerwin. "Interest Group Participation in Rule Making: A Decade of Change." *Journal of Public Administration Research and Theory* 15, no. 3 (2004): 353–70.

Haider, Donald. "Grants as a Tool of Public Policy." In *Beyond Privatization: The Tools of Government Action*, edited by Lester M. Salamon, 93–124. Washington, DC: Urban Institute, 1989.

Hofmann, Eva, Katharina Gangl, Erich Kirchler, and Jennifer Stark. "Enhancing Tax Compliance through Coercive and Legitimate Power of Tax Authorities by Concurrently Diminishing or Facilitating Trust in Tax Authorities." *Law & Policy* 36, no. 3 (July 2014): 290–313.

Hood, Christopher. *The Tools of Government*. Chatham: Chatham House Publishers, 1986.

Howard, Christopher. *The Hidden Welfare State: Tax Expenditures and Social Policy in the United States*. Princeton, NJ: Princeton University Press, 1997.

Howlett, Michael, and Andrea Migone. "The Permanence of Temporary Services: The Reliance of Canadian Federal Departments on Policy and Management Consultants." *Canadian Public Administration* 56, no. 3 (2013): 369–90.

Hudson, John, Stuart Lowe, Natalie Oscroft, and Carolyn Snell. "Activating Policy Networks: A Case Study of Local Environmental Policy-Making in the United Kingdom." *Policy Studies* 28, no. 1 (2007): 55–70.

Kash, Jeffrey P. "Enemies to Allies: The Role of Policy-Design Aadaptation in Facilitating a Farmer-Environmentalist Alliance." *Policy Studies Journal* 36, no. 1 (2008): 39–60.

King, David C. "The Origins and Maintenance of Groups." In *Mobilizing Interest Groups in America: Patrons, Professions and Social Movements*, edited by Jack L. Walker, 75–102. Ann Arbor: University of Michigan Press, 1991.

Klitgaard, Michael Baggesen. "School Vouchers and the New Politics of the Welfare State." *Governance* 21, no. 4 (2008): 479–98.

Leeuw, Frans L. "The Carrot: Subsidies as a Tool of Government." In *Carrots, Sticks and Sermons: Policy Instruments and Their Evaluation*, edited by Bemelmans-Videc, Mary-Louise, Ray C. Rist, and Evert Vedung, Evert, 77–102. New Brunswick, NJ: Transaction Publishers, 1998.

Lowry, Robert C. "Foundation Patronage toward Citizen Groups and Think Tank: Who Gets Grants?" *The Journal of Politics* 81, no. 3 (1999): 758–76.

Lybecker, Kristina M., and Robert A. Freeman. "Funding Pharmaceutical Innovation through Direct Tax Credits." *Health Economics, Politics and Law* 2, no. 3 (2007): 267–84.

Mahoney, Christine, and Michael Joseph Beckstrand. "Following the Money: EU Funding of Civil Society Organizations." Potsdam, 2009.

Maslove, Allan M. "Loans and Loan Guarantees: Business as Usual Versus the Politics of Risk." In *How Ottawa Spends: The Liberals, The Opposition and Federal Priorities*, edited by G. Bruce Doern, 121–32. Toronto, ON: James Lorimer, 1983.

Maslove, Allan M. "The Other Side of Public Spending: Tax Expenditures in Canada." In *The Public Evaluation of Government Spending*, edited by G. Bruce Doern and Allan M. Maslove, 149–68. Toronto, ON: Butterworth, 1979.

McCrudden, Christopher. "Using Public Procurement to Achieve Social Outcomes." *Natural Resources Journal* 28 (2004): 257–67.

Nowlan, David M. "Local Taxation as an Instrument of Policy." In *The Changing Canadian Metropolis: A Public Policy Perspective*, edited by Frances Frisken, 799–841. Berkeley, CA: Institute of Governmental Studies, 1994.

Nownes, Anthony J. "The Population Ecology of Interest Group Formation: Mobilizing for Gay and Lesbian Rights in the United States, 1950–98." *British Journal of Political Science* 34, no. 1 (2004): 49–67.

Nownes, Anthony, and Grant Neeley. "Toward an Explanation for Public Interest Group Formation and Proliferation: 'Seed Money', Disturbances, Entrepreneurship, and Patronage." *Policy Studies Journal* 24, no. 1 (1996): 74–92.

Olson, Mancur. *The Logic of Collective Action: Public Goods and the Theory of Groups*. Cambridge, MA: Harvard University Press, 1965.

Pal, Leslie A. *Interests of State: The Politics of Language, Multiculturalism, and Feminism in Canada*. Montreal, QC: McGill-Queen's University Press, 1993.

Phillips, Susan. "Meaning and Structure in Social Movements: Mapping the Network of National Canadian Women's Organizations." *Canadian Journal of Political Science* 24, no. 4 (1991): 755–82.

Phillips, Susan, and Tessa Hebb. "Financing the Third Sector: Introduction." *Policy and Society* 29, no. 3 (August 2010): 181–87.

Pope, Jeff, and Anthony D. Owen. "Emission Trading Schemes: Potential Revenue Effects, Compliance Costs and Overall Tax Policy Issues." *Energy Policy* 37 (2009): 4595–603.

Rich, Andrew. *Think Tanks, Public Policy, and the Politics of Expertise*. New York: Cambridge University Press, 2004.

Rolfstam, Max. "Public Procurement as an Innovation Policy Tool: The Role of Institutions." *Science and Public Policy* 36, no. 5 (2009): 349–60.

Schmitter, Philippe C. "Modes of Interest Intermediation and Models of Societal Change in Western Europe." *Comparative Political Studies* 10, no. 1 (1977): 7–38.

Stanbury, William T. "A Skeptic's Guide to the Claims of So-Called Public Interest Groups." *Canadian Public Administration* 36, no. 4 (1993): 580–605.

Stasiulis, Daiva K. "The Symbolic Mosaic Reaffirmed: Multiculturalilsm Policy." In *How Ottawa Spends 1988/89: The Conservatives Heading into the Stretch*, edited by Katherine A. Graham, 81–111. Ottawa, ON: Carleton University Press, 1988.

Strolovitch, Dara Z. "Do Interest Groups Represent the Disadvantaged? Advocacy at the Intersections of Race, Class and Gender." *The Journal of Politics* 68, no. 4 (2006): 894–910.

Sunnevag, Kjell J. "Designing Auctions for Offshore Petroleum Lease Allocation." *Resources Policy* 26 (2000): 3–16.

Surrey, Stanley S. "Tax Incentives as a Device for Implementing Government Policy: A Comparison with Direct Government Expenditures." *Harvard Law Review* 83, no. 4 (February 1, 1970): 705–38.

Toke, David. "Policy Network Creation: The Case of Energy Efficiency." *Public Administration* 78, no. 4 (2000): 835–54.

Valkama, Pekka, and Stephen J. Bailey. "Vouchers as an Alternative Public Sector Funding System." *Public Policy and Administration* 16, no. 1 (2001): 32–58.

Walker, Jack L. *Mobilizing Interest Groups in America: Patrons, Professions and Social Movements.* Ann Arbor: University of Michigan Press, 1991.

Woodside, Ken. "Tax Incentives vs. Subsidies: Political Considerations in Governmental Choice." *Canadian Public Policy* 5, no. 2 (1979): 248–56.

6 Information-based implementation tools

Information-based tools are those based on the last of the four categories of resources set out by Hood (1986): 'nodality' or 'centrality' or, as defined in Chapter 1, involved in communicating 'knowledge' or 'information' to target groups or collecting it from them in the expectation that this will alter their behaviour or better inform government policy-making. These are the 'sermon' in the 'carrots, sticks and sermons' formulation of policy instruments, alongside the 'carrot' of financial tools and the 'stick' or authority-based ones.

As Evert Vedung defines them, information-based policy tools are 'efforts to use the knowledge and data available to governments to influence consumer and producer behaviour in a direction consistent with government aims and wishes and/or gather information in order to further their aims and ambitions' (Vedung and van der Doelen 1998).

Exactly what is meant by the term 'information' or 'communication' varies from author to author, ranging from its association with all forms of political activity to a very specific focus on one type of action, like public service or political advertising (Firestone 1970). It is also important to note that many new communication practices have emerged in recent years, at least in part due to the development of new information technologies, notably computerization, the internet and the rise of social media, which have broadened the range and menu of government nodality tools (Feldman and Khademian 2007). These include the development and use of instruments which promote citizen empowerment such as freedom of information (FOI) legislation, the use of public performance measures, various forms of e- or 'digital' government and the increased use of government surveys and advertising including in the use of platforms such as Twitter or Facebook, amongst others (Margetts and Sutcliffe 2013).

And this definition, while useful, is limited in that it conceals or elides the two different general purposes to which these resources can be put. These are the familiar procedural versus substantive distinction used throughout this book – whether these activities are intended to serve as devices primarily oriented towards the manipulation of the behaviour of policy actors in policy processes or as social and economic ones involved in and affecting the production, distribution and consumption of different types of goods and services (Jahn et al. 2005). Disentangling the two is necessary in order to provide a clearer analysis of the role each plays in policy designs.

Substantive informational instruments

Following Vedung's lead, we can define substantive government communication policy instruments as those policy techniques or mechanisms which rely on the use of information to directly or indirectly affect the behaviour of those involved in the production, consumption and distribution of different kinds of goods and services in society. As Hood (1986) noted, these kinds of tools can be targeted at different levels of society – individuals, groups and populations as a whole and according to whether they are intended to collect or disseminate information.

The most high profile and thus most commonly observed and chronicled type of substantive implementation tool is the instrument focused on the effort to alter consumer behaviour: the *government information campaign* (Hornik 1989). This includes various campaigns waged by governments to encourage citizens to, for example, eat well, drink less, exercize more and generally engage in fewer vices and otherwise behave more responsibly, which are common in many countries. Communication activities aimed at altering producer behaviour through provision of product and process information to customers (*labelling and product information*) are also very prominent (Jahn et al. 2005).

Information dissemination tools

Information dissemination tools like public service advertising are classic 'persuasion instruments' and are the most studied substantive information-based implementation tools. Adler and Pittle define these instruments as those 'persuasion schemes [which] convey messages which may or may not contain factual information which overtly seek to motivate target audiences to modify their behaviour' (Adler and Pittle 1984: 160). These tools are used often, as they are fairly inexpensive. However, they remain controversial, as the line between communications and intrusive propaganda is one which is easily blurred and, like all advertizing of any kind, their effectiveness is difficult to gauge (Gelders and Ihlen 2010).

Exhortation and moral suasion

The most prominent type of substantive information tool designed to persuade is the appeal from political leaders to various social actors, urging them to follow a government's lead in some area of social or economic life. Stanbury and Fulton (1984) provide a list of 'exhortation' and 'moral suasion' activities, which include 'pure political leadership such as appeals for calm, better behaviour, high principles and whereby voluntary action is urged under threat of coercion if refused' (304).

Such forms of 'moral suasion' are often specifically aimed or targeted at individual producers or sectors and are typically used within the context of an already existing regulatory regime. These can help governments regulate a variety of activities without necessarily creating new legal instruments in order to do so. Many countries, for example, administer important aspects of their financial systems in this fashion, asking banks, taxpayers and other financial institutions to act in a certain way (e.g. keep interest rates low, or allow certain groups to borrow funds, or not engage in risky lending or borrowing behaviour), with the implicit or explicit threat of direct government regulation if such requests are ignored or go unfulfilled (Bardach 1989). Government requests are often very focused and can be quite secretive (for example, in the immediate aftermath of the 9/11 airline hijackings when the US government urged credit card companies to provide records of suspicious activities by suspected hijackers and most complied).

Information campaigns

Mass media and targeted information campaigns, on the other hand, are much more visible, by definition, and tend to be aimed less at producers than at consumers (Hornik 1989). Adler and Pittle (1984) describe these tools as 'notification instruments' which 'convey factual information to the intelligent target. Implicit in the notification approach is the belief that the target, once apprised of the facts, will make the appropriate decision'.

Some notification tools do attempt to be purely factual, ongoing and passive in nature, such as nutritional labelling on foodstuffs or health warnings on cigarettes (Padberg 1992; Baksi and Bose 2007). They are usually enacted in regulations (i.e. disclosure is mandatory) and are aimed at providing information to consumers allowing them to make better decisions, or overcome information asymmetries between producers and consumers, with the expectation that consumers will change their behaviour in some way consistent with government goals – for example, reducing smoking, exercising more or eating nutritional foods rather than snacks (Jahn et al. 2005). Although the evidence of the effectiveness of such campaigns is mixed (Mann and Wustemann 2010; Barreiro-Hurlé et al. 2010), this has not dampened their growth.

Other information campaigns are more active and less factual, but have the same intent, that is, providing social actors with more information about aspects of their behaviour and its advantageous or deleterious quality, urging enhancement of the former and diminishment of the latter. The information transmitted through such information instruments is not always so factual, however, but can be used to 'sell' a government's policies in the same way that other products are marketed (Rothschild 1979). Such campaigns are often conducted at the mass level and use a variety of mass-media delivery mechanisms (commercials, broadcasts, newspaper and social media advertisements and the like). High-profile campaigns in many countries to prevent drinking and driving or those that encourage the purchase of war bonds during wartime are good examples of the use of this kind of instrument.

This kind of mass campaign began with the emergence of mass media and is now common in most countries, including in most cases an extensive social media component. Many national governments are now the largest purchasers of advertising in their countries and far outstrip national brands well known for their advertising overkill, such as alcoholic beverage, soft drink companies as well as fast food chains. The federal government of Canada, for example, has been the largest advertiser in the country since 1976 (Stanbury et al. 1983), with the larger provincial governments in the top ten as well. Ryan (1995) noted that federal advertising expanded from $3.4 million in 1968, to $106.5 million in 1992, a 3,000 per cent increase. Even inflation adjusted this amounted to a 665 per cent increase in 25 years.

Although they can be costly, such campaigns are generally less expensive than many other alternatives, although the costs of non-compliance must also be taken into account (Pellikaan and van der Veen 2002). Generally, governments will tend to include information tools and government communications in policy designs only when:

1   100 per cent compliance is not required for a policy to be effective,
2   government and public interests coincide (e.g. on health awareness) so that government appeals are likely to be favourably received and
3   a relatively short-term crisis situation exists when other tools may require too much lead time to be effective; where
4   it is otherwise difficult to impose sanctions and where
5   the issue in question is not very complex (technological or legal) in nature but can be reduced to the level of advertising slogans (Rose 1993)

Nudges and information-based choice architectures

In recent years, much attention has been paid to another similar use of information provision as a governing tool which operates on a less conscious basis. Growth in this kind of tool use has occurred largely as a result of work in psychology and behavioural economics which has identified and promoted the use of different kinds of 'nudges' or cues to encourage or discourage certain kinds of behaviour, mainly in individuals and most often on a semi- or sub-conscious level (Thaler and Sunstein2009). These cues are more subtle than traditional information and media-based campaigns, and are often targeted at the unconscious or semi-conscious level of individual behaviour or what has been called "system 1" thinking ("fast, emotional, semi-rational thinking to distinguish it from more deliberative and rational 'system 2'" thinking (Kahneman 2013). These can include such micro-level interventions as changing the default opt-in on organ donation forms to a default opt-out for example, or painting walking path lines in subway stations that lead to stairs rather than escalators in order to encourage exercise.

Sunstein (2015) identified ten important types of such "nudges". They are all efforts to alter citizen behaviour by altering the informational environment in which they operate through activation of 'system 1' or quasi-automatic cognitive responses. These include:

 i Changing default rules such as making people opt out rather than in to some scheme,
 ii Simplification of the options presented to individuals, such as a shortened contract,
 iii Use of social norms to encourage people to conform to certain practices, such as not littering or jaywalking,
 iv Increases in ease and convenience such as making bike paths and exercise areas common and easily accessible,
 v Disclosure, that is, mandating the provision of certain kinds of information, like the real interest rate charged to credit card debt,
 vi Warnings, graphic or otherwise, to discourage behaviour, such as mandatory pictures of cancer victims on cigarette packages,
 vii Pre-commitment strategies such as the provision of peer-supported anti-obesity or alcoholism support groups such as Weight Watchers or Alcoholics Anonymous,
 viii Reminders of important activities such as children's dental appointment or vaccination schedules,
 ix Eliciting implementation intentions through various campaigns such as voter registration drives or pension planning and

x Informing people of the nature and consequences of their own past choices such as informing them of the amount they have spent on electricity in past months or years on their current bill.

Many of these items deal with the design of bills, forms or mailings of various kinds and are intended to provide use and cost information about their behaviour to consumers, which might otherwise be difficult or impossible for them to collect and which might alter their behaviour, such as revealing what is their water or electricity use compared to their neighbours.

Although the idea of 'nudging' received a surge of attention in recent years, the effectiveness of such measures remains unclear as does their application. Evidence suggests, for example, that they may have a role to play in solving large-scale policy issues such as energy conservation but only when they are exercised in tandem with other policy tools such as financial incentives or penalties (Schubert 2017). And their impact appears to vary by country and target population.

Moreover, there may be an unintended 'behavioural spillover' of nudges (Galizzi 2014). That is, there is a risk of infantilizing and diminishing people's autonomous decision-making capacities by constantly manipulating them, as happened often in the business world around, for example, multiple subtle changes to mobile phone plans. They are also subject to diminishing returns and also to a concern regarding the potential for abuse in the use of nudging to shape people's choices in pro-government ways (Hausman and Welch 2010). Governments may also be unable to counter 'nudge'-style tactics employed by private market institutions which, for example, encourage people to spend rather than save, or smoke or gamble rather than abstain, to name only a few.

Hagman et al. (2015) also find significant differences in the receptiveness of different populations to nudging activity. They find a high degree of acceptance towards 'nudge' policies among a sample population drawn from Sweden and the United States, but also a majority of the respondents perceiving such policies to be intrusive to their freedom of choice. Policies that the researchers classified as pro-social (i.e. focusing on social welfare) had a significantly lower acceptance rate compared to pro-self nudge policies (i.e. focusing on private welfare). In addition, 'overt' nudges, that is, those that target conscious, higher-order cognitive processes of decision-making were preferred by people over 'covert' nudges (i.e. those that target subconscious, lower-order processes of decision-making). (Felsen et al. 2013).

Regardless of the information-based behavioural tool being employed, whether a nudge, shove or budge, in cases where incentives for non-compliance are high, such information-based tools may be unlikely to secure compliance by themselves. In such cases, policy-makers need to think about both the barriers that may be preventing compliance and how to match a variety of policy tools to the most important barriers, taking into account the heterogeneity within the given population in terms of their receptiveness to different tool uses.

Information and knowledge collection tools

Information collection is the key to many and better policies (Nutley et al. 2007), and many implementation instruments exist to collect information for governments and can contribute to enhanced 'evidence-based' policy-making. This extends to the use of licensing provisions in which information may be collected before or after a licence is granted, but can also involve the use of research and generation of new policy-relevant knowledge through special forums such as inquiries and commissions.

Inquiries and commissions

One fairly common and high-profile means by which governments collect information is the use of official inquiries such as a judicial inquiry or executive commission. As discussed in previous chapters, these exist on a spectrum depending on their relationship to government agencies and according to their functions. Some inquiries and task forces are largely internal to government and intended to mobilize network actors. Other kinds of commissions, however, are designed primarily to collect information (Rowe and McAllister 2006).

Many judicial inquiries fall into this category and have a great deal of autonomy from governments. They are a common feature of many governments and enjoy a variety of different relationships with their commissioners. Presidential and royal commissions, for example, are independent and autonomous, although they still depend on government for budgets and resources. Others are less 'arms-length' and expected to report back to specific agencies on specific subjects, with no guarantee that their reports will ever be released to the public. All of these devices can be used to summarize existing knowledge or generate new data on a subject (Sheriff 1983).

Statistical agencies and units

Another such information collection and dissemination tool is the use of statistical agencies which are specifically tasked with collecting data on a wide variety of social activities of individuals, groups and firms.

These typically operate using internationally recognized standards for classifying these activities and may rely more or less heavily on voluntary disclosure of information. These agencies may conduct surveys on specialized topics and/or periodic censuses of national or subnational populations (Anderson and Whitford 2018).

This information is often used to determine such factors as the level of per capita grants transferred between governments, or the number and types of hospitals and medical facilities which should be built and where these, and other public institutions like schools and offices, should be located. National and other-level statistical agencies are expensive to establish and maintain, but once in operation, they can be used to collect information on many subjects at relatively low cost and often provide otherwise very hard-to-collect information to the public as well as governments through, for example, time series databases on a wide range of issues from housing to consumer savings rates.

Surveys and polling

In many countries, governments are now the largest purchasers of surveys (Hastak et al. 2001), and many government agencies now undertake surveys on a regular basis, as environmental scans both in order to try to anticipate issues, and in order to determine public opinion on agency performance (Rothmayr and Hardmeier 2002; Page 2006). These include activities from in-person focus groups to traditional telephone surveys to various kinds of topic modeling and sentiment analysis linked to social media use. Governments are major users of all of these media and techniques and use the information collected both to alter and inform their policy designs and improve their implementation.

Procedural informational instruments

In order to pursue their preferred policy initiatives, governments can also use procedural tools based on government information resources in order to attempt to alter the behaviour of policy actors involved in policy-making processes, just as they attempt to alter consumer and producer behaviour through the employment of substantive information-based tools (Burris et al. 2005).

Information-based procedural implementation tools are those designed to affect policy processes in a way consistent with government aims and ambitions through the control and selective provision of information. These are 'nodality' instruments, as Hood (1986) noted, because the information exchanged is valuable largely as a function of the government's position as a key nodal link in a policy network. Some of these efforts are aimed at promoting information release, while others are aimed at preventing it.

Both European and American studies have found that governments have increasingly employed a variety of these procedural information-based instruments to indirectly affect the outcomes of the policy process in ways that are consistent with their aims and objectives (Johansson and Borell 1999). The most commonly observed and chronicled category of procedural tool is the type which focuses on the use of *general information prevention or disclosure laws* and other tools – such as access to information laws – in order to provide policy network actors with the knowledge required to effectively filter and focus their demands on government for new policy measures or reforms to older ones. However, governments are also very much involved in the use of communications on government websites and through other means (Hood and Margetts 2007) to provide additional information to policy network members in specific sectoral or issue areas in order to both enhance their credibility and effectiveness but also to promote specific kinds of policy-making such as evidence-based rather than pure advocacy activity.

Information release tools

Stanbury and Fulton (1984) describe two common types of procedural information release or disclosure tools: *information disclosure* (for example, through formal freedom of information and privacy laws) and *consultation/co-optation tools*, like public hearings, the discreet use of confidential information such as planned leaks to the press or planned public disclosure of government intentions.

Freedom of information and E- or digital government legislation and other initiatives

FOI provisions allow access to an individual's own records and those of others – with numerous exemptions to protect, for example, trade secrets, individual privacy or national security. Many of these exemptions are benign (to protect other individuals from unnecessary disclosure) and allowing access to documents and records of others – with numerous exemptions – again many benign and intended to protect individuals from unnecessary disclosure. These legislative arrangements were a feature of the centuries-old Scandinavian ombudsman system of administrative control, for example, which attempted to provide information to citizens on what a government was doing and then also provide a specialized office – the ombudsman – to allow citizens to pursue complaints based on that information. These were introduced in many other countries in the 1970s and the 1980s (Bennett and Raab 2003) and are sometimes accompanied by 'whistleblower' acts, that is, bills intended to protect people who speak out about problems in the government's bureaucracy. Through such legislation, bureaucrats and employees are often offered legal protection against reprisals for reporting government wrongdoing. Both represent popular forms of procedural information tool design.

Various kinds of open data and e-government projects, often referred to collectively as 'digital government', which move previously in-person service delivery online, also often have an information release component to them, collecting data on users or providing additional venues for users to obtain information on government programmes and other options which can help to better inform their policy delibera-tions, evaluations and discourses (Clarke et al. 2017).

Information release prevention tools

There is also a wide range of these kinds of tools designed to protect certain kinds of information on government activities or in government files and prevent its distribution to the public. These include protecting not only information collected by governments but that which comes into their possession (for example, from a foreign government or via documents filed in court cases, and the like). These range from bans on political parties and speech such as hate crimes legislation, to official secrets acts with various levels of confidentiality and penalties imposed for publicizing or releasing government secrets, especially, but not exclu-sively, around areas such as national security. These kinds of tools exist in every policy domain and are included in or effect every policy design.

Censorship

This has occurred in many countries during wartime but also in peacetime, for example, as media, film or theatre censorship. This latter use has been slowly whittled away in most advanced countries, as indi-vidual rights in democratic states have been ruled to trump government or collective ones, but wartime prohibitions of this kind remain very common (Qualter 1985).

Official secrets acts

Official secrets acts are a replacement for censorship in many areas of government activity. They are often the most important statute relating to national security in many countries and are designed to prohibit and control access to, and the disclosure of, sensitive government information (Pasquier and Villeneuve 2007). Offences tend to cover espionage and leakage of government information. The term 'official secret' varies dramatically in meaning from country to country, but, broadly, allows governments to classify documents and prohibit release of different categories for sometimes very long periods (e.g. 50–75 years) if not forever. All countries have some form of official secrecy, although the legislative and executive basis for such laws varies quite dramatically between countries.

Privacy and data protection acts

These acts exist in many jurisdictions as a counterpoint to access to information laws in which various types of personally specific information is excluded from such acts. Some jurisdictions have specific legislation devoted to this subject, usually with a focus on protecting personal information in areas such as health, financial or tax matters and with respect to criminal proceedings (Bennett and Raab 2003).

These instruments are also quite varied, but, in general, it is fair to say that restricting information is low cost to initiate, but high cost to monitor and maintain, while the reverse is true of information disclosure. In terms of targeting, it is true of both sets of instruments that it is very difficult to target either secrecy or disclosure on specific groups. As a result, these actions are typically more difficult to set up and take more time and effort than is often thought to be the case, although they remain a frequent component of many policy designs especially in sensitive areas such as health.

Conclusion: information – cost-efficient but often ineffective

As has been described earlier, there are many different kinds of government communication and information activities, and in the past the lack of an effective taxonomy or framework for their analysis has made generalizing about their impact and patterns of use quite difficult. Describing information-based policy tools in the terms set out earlier helps to highlight the similarities and differences between different instruments and helps develop a relatively parsimonious classification of their major types which can facilitate national and cross-national studies of their use and impact.

Information dissemination activities remain relatively low cost in terms of financial and personnel outlays, but compliance is a major issue and, as in all advertising activities, evaluating the impact of these campaigns is very uncertain (Salmon 1989a, b). Adler and Pittle (1984: 161), for example, found 'many of these programs require more careful planning, larger expenditures and longer implementation periods than they usually receive'.

The assumption that greater knowledge always equals greater compliance with government aims, for example, is not always the case. Alcoholism and drug abuse, for instance, are complex problems that are not 'rational' in the sense that individuals continue to consume or engage in them while knowing fullwell their destructive attributes (so-called 'demerit goods') (Weiss and Tschirhart 1994) and greater knowledge may not affect or alter behaviour in such cases.

Thus, while it may be the dream of many governments that simply monitoring and communicating with people will accomplish all of their ends, this is not usually the case. The benefits to government in using such tools, including the more recently described 'nudges' and 'choice architectures' they deploy, may thus be much lower than anticipated if such a high visibility instrument is perceived to have failed and the blame for a continuing policy problem is focused squarely on governments (Hood 2007). Such considerations are a prominent feature in the design of policy alternatives envisioning the use of such tools, often resulting in their use in combination with other tools rather than as the sole tool deployed in a policy area of interest.

References

Anderson, Derrick M., and Andrew Whitford. "Designing Systems for the Co-Production of Public Knowledge: Considerations for National Statistical Systems." *Policy Design and Practice* 1, no. 1 (January 2, 2018): 79–89.

Baksi, Soham, and Pinaki Bose. "Credence Goods, Efficient Labeling Policies, and Regulatory Enforcement." *Environmental and Resource Economics* 37 (2007): 411–30.

Bardach, E., and L. M. Salamon. "Social Regulation as a Generic Policy Instrument." In *Beyond Privatization: The Tools of Government Action*, edited by L. M. Salamon, 197–229. Washington, DC: Urban Institute, 1989.

Barreiro-Hurlé, Jesús, Azucena Gracia, and Tiziana de-Magistris. "Does Nutrition Information on Food Products Lead to Healthier Food Choices?" *Food Policy* 35, no. 3 (June 2010): 221–29.

Bennett, C. J., and C. D. Raab. *The Governance of Privacy: Policy Instruments in Global Perspective*. Aldershot: Ashgate, 2003.

Burris, Scott, Peter Drahos, and Clifford Shearing. "Nodal Governance." *Australian Journal of Legal Philosophy* 30 (2005): 30.

Clarke, Amanda, Evert A. Lindquist, and Jeffrey Roy. "Understanding Governance in the Digital Era: An Agenda for Public Administration Research in Canada." *Canadian Public Administration* 60, no. 4 (December 1, 2017): 457–75.

Feldman, Martha S., and Anne M. Khademian. "The Role of the Public Manager in Inclusion: Creating Communities of Participation." *Governance* 20, no. 2 (2007): 305–24.

Felsen, Gidon, Noah Castelo, and Peter B. Reiner. "Decisional Enhancement and Autonomy: Public Attitudes towards Overt and Covert Nudges." *Judgment and Decision Making* 8, no. 3 (2013): 202–13.

Firestone, O. J. *The Public Persuader: Government Advertising.* Toronto, ON: Methuen, 1970.

Galizzi, Matteo M. "What Is Really Behavioral in Behavioral Health Policy? And Does It Work?" *Applied Economic Perspectives and Policy* 36, no. 1 (March 1, 2014): 25–60.

Gelders, Dave, and Øyvind Ihlen. "Government Communication about Potential Policies: Public Relations, Propaganda or Both?" *Public Relations Review* 36, no. 1 (March 2010): 59–62.

Hagman, William, David Andersson, Daniel Västfjäll, and Gustav Tinghög. "Public Views on Policies Involving Nudges." *Review of Philosophy and Psychology* 6, no. 3 (May 28, 2015): 439–53.

Hastak, M., M. B. Mazis, and L. A. Morris. "The Role of Consumer Surveys in Public Policy Decision Making." *Journal of Public Policy and Marketing* 20, no. 2 (2001): 170–85.

Hausman, Daniel M., and Brynn Welch. "Debate: To Nudge or Not to Nudge★." *Journal of Political Philosophy* 18, no. 1 (March 1, 2010): 123–36.

Hood, Christopher. *The Tools of Government.* Chatham: Chatham House Publishers, 1986.

Hood, Christopher. "What Happens When Transparency Meets Blame-Avoidance?" *Public Management Review* 9, no. 2 (2007): 191–210.

Hood, Christopher, and Helen Z. Margetts. *The Tools of Government in the Digital Age.* Basingstoke: Palgrave Macmillan, 2007.

Hornik, R. "The Knowledge-Behavior Gap in Public Information Campaigns." In *Information Campaigns: Managing the Process of Social Change*, edited by C. Salmon. Newbury Park, CA: Sage, 1989: 219–37.

Jahn, G., M. Schramm, and A. Spiller. "The Reliability of Certification: Quality Labels as a Consumer Policy Tool." *Journal of Consumer Policy* 28 (2005): 53–73.

Johansson, R., and K. Borell. "Central Steering and Local Networks: Old-Age Care in Sweden." *Public Administration* 77, no. 3 (1999): 585–98.

Kahneman, Daniel. *Thinking, Fast and Slow.* New York: Farrar, Straus and Giroux, 2013.

Mann, Stefan, and Henry Wustemann. "Public Governance of Information Asymmetries: The Gap between Reality and Economic Theory." *The Journal of Socio-Economics* 39, no. 2 (2010): 278–85.

Margetts, Helen, and David Sutcliffe. "Addressing the Policy Challenges and Opportunities of 'Big Data.'" *Policy & Internet* 5, no. 2 (June 1, 2013): 139–46.

Nutley, Sandra M., Isabel Walter, and Huw T. O. Davies. *Using Evidence: How Research Can Inform Public Services.* Bristol: Policy Press, 2007.

Padberg, D. I. "Nutritional Labeling as a Policy Instrument." *American Journal of Agricultural Economics* 74, no. 5 (1992): 1208–13.

Page, Christopher. *The Roles of Public Opinion Research in Canadian Government.* Toronto: University of Toronto Press, 2006.

Pasquier, Martial, and Jean-Patrick Villeneuve. "Organizational Barriers to Transparency: A Typology and Analysis of Organizational Behaviour Tending to Prevent of Restrict Access to Information." *International Review of Administrative Sciences* 73, no. 1 (2007): 147–62.

Pellikaan, Huib, and Robert J. van der Veen. *Environmental Dilemmas and Policy Design.* Cambridge: Cambridge University Press, 2002.

Qualter, T. H. *Opinion Control in the Democracies.* London: Macmillan, 1985.

Robert S. Adler and R. David Pittle. "Cajolry or Command: Are Education Campaigns an Adequate Substitute for Regulation?" *Yale Journal on Regulation* 1, no. 2 (1984): 159–93.

Rose, J. "Government Advertising in a Crisis: The Quebec Referendum Precedent." *Canadian Journal of Communication* 18 (1993): 173–96.

Rothmayr, C., and S. Hardmeier. "Government and Polling: Use and Impact of Polls in the Policy-Making Process in Switzerland." *International Journal of Public Opinion Research* 14, no. 2 (2002): 123–40.

Rothschild, M. L. "Marketing Communications in Nonbusiness Situations or Why It's So Hard to Sell Brotherhood Like Soap." *Journal of Marketing* 43, no. Spring (1979): 11–20.

Rowe, Mike, and Laura McAllister. "The Roles of Commissions of Inquiry in the Policy Process." *Public Policy and Administration* 21, no. 4 (December 1, 2006): 99–115.

Ryan, P. "Miniature Mila and Flying Geese: Government Advertising and Canadian Democracy." In *How Ottawa Spends 1995–96: Mid-Life Crises*, edited by S. D. Phillips, 263–86. Ottawa, ON: Carleton University Press, 1995.

Salmon, C. "Campaigns for Social Improvement: An Overview of Values, Rationales, and Impacts." In *Information Campaigns: Managing the Process of Social Change*, edited by C. Salmon, 1–32. Newbury Park, CA: Sage, 1989a.

Salmon, C. *Information Campaigns: Managing the Process of Social Change.* Newbury Park, CA: Sage, 1989b.

Schubert, Christian. "Green Nudges: Do They Work? Are They Ethical?" *Ecological Economics* 132, no. Supplement C (February 1, 2017): 329–42.

Sheriff, P. E. "State Theory, Social Science, and Governmental Commissions." *American Behavioural Scientist* 26, no. 5 (1983): 669–80.

Stanbury, W. T., and J. Fulton. "Suasion as a Governing Instrument." In *How Ottawa Spends 1984: The New Agenda*, edited by A. Maslove, 282–324. Toronto, ON: Lorimer, 1984.

Stanbury, W. T., G. J. Gorn, and C. B. Weinberg. "Federal Advertising Expenditures." In *How Ottawa Spends: The Liberals, the Opposition and Federal Priorities*, edited by G. B. Doern, 133–72. Toronto, ON: James Lorimer and Company, 1983.

Sunstein, Cass R. *Why Nudge? The Politics of Libertarian Paternalism*. Reprint edition. New Haven, CT: Yale University Press, 2015.

Thaler, Richard H., and Cass R. Sunstein. *Nudge: Improving Decisions about Health, Wealth, and Happiness*. Revised & Expanded edition. New York: Penguin Books, 2009.

Vedung, E., and Frans C. J. van der Doelen. "The Sermon: Information Programs in the Public Policy Process – Choice, Effects and Evaluation." In *Carrots, Sticks and Sermons: Policy Instruments and Their Evaluation*, edited by M. L. Bemelmans-Videc and R. C. Rist, 103–28. New Brunswick, NJ: Transaction Publishers, 1998.

Weiss, J. A., and M. Tschirhart. "Public Information Campaigns as Policy Instruments." *Journal of Policy Analysis and Management* 13, no. 1 (1994): 82–119.

Part III

Principles for designing policies and programmes

7 Assembling and evaluating an effective policy design

As was pointed out in the Introduction to this book, the pioneers of policy design research in the 1980s and the 1990s argued that like other kinds of design activities in fields such as manufacturing and construction, policy design involves (1) knowledge of the basic building blocks or materials with which actors must work in constructing a (policy) object, (2) knowledge of the construction process itself and (3) the elaboration of a set of principles regarding how materials should be combined in that construction (Schon 1984). A superior policy design, then, is, at least in part, a matter of determining the parameters of a given policy situation and of matching the needs for action, with the supply of tools available, tasks which can be done well ('good' design) or poorly ('poor' design).

In a policy context, this means understanding the kinds of implementation tools governments have at their disposal in attempting to alter some aspect of society and societal behaviour set out in Chapters 3–6 and elaborating a set of principles concerning which instruments should be used in which circumstances. It is to the second and third task that this chapter is devoted.

What makes a good policy process: evidence-based policy-making, policy analytical capacity and their links to good policy design

As set out Chapter 1, all design efforts are based on theoretically informed empirical analyses, through which it is expected that governments can learn from experience and avoid repeating the errors of the past, as well as better apply new techniques to the resolution of old and new problems (Sanderson 2002). Not all policies go through this process but such evidence-based or 'evidence-informed' policy efforts represent an effort to structure policy processes in such a way as to minimize non-design spaces and incidences by prioritizing evidentiary decision-making criteria and capacities. This is done in the expectation that superior policies and results will emerge from such processes than from 'non-design' ones (Head, 2016).

Attaining this standard of policy-making is not automatic, however, but requires a high level of what Riddell (1998) termed 'policy research capacity'. He summarized the requisites of this analytical capacity as lying in:

> a recognized requirement or demand for research; a supply of qualified researchers; ready availability of quality data; policies and procedures to facilitate productive interactions with other researchers; and a culture in which openness is encouraged and risk taking is acceptable.

That is, for evidence-based policy-making to be achieved, policy actors, including governments, require both the desire and the ability to collect, aggregate, communicate and apply information in order to effectively develop medium- and long-term projections, proposals for and evaluations of future government activities. Organizations both inside and outside of governments require a high level of human, financial, network and knowledge resources in order to enable them to perform the tasks associated with managing and implementing such an evidence-based policy process.

But, even in the best of circumstances and with the best of intentions, governments often grapple with complex problems involving situations in which they must deal with multiple actors, ideas and interests in uncertain and complex problem environments which typically evolve and change over time. And, as Chapter 2 discussed, in many other instances governments may lack the intention to proceed deliberately through the development and evaluation of policy analysis and policy decisions and design considerations may be more or less absent from policy deliberations. Policy formulators or decision-makers, for example, may not have access to the kinds of types of information they need to design effective policies or may engage in purely interest-driven trade-offs or legislative or bureaucratic log-rolling between different values or resource uses which negates whatever evidence they may have at their disposal. Or, more extremely, they may engage in venal or corrupt behaviour in which personal or partisan gain from a decision may trump all other evaluative criteria regardless of the nature of the policy development process followed.

That having been said though, most governments have at one point or another encountered poor results from non-evidence-based or weak evidence-based policy processes which led to easily avoidable and forseeable errors and policy failures and most desire to enhance their capacity and improve their formulation processes, moving into a more positive design space whenever possible (Gleeson et al. 2011). This involves them in identifying the potential use of a variety of tools such as those set out in Chapters 3–6, and the use of analysis in the effort to better match the potential of each tool to fit the job at hand.

What is a superior mix of tools: coherence, consistency and congruence in policy designs

Having a superior policy-making process, however, tells us little about how a mix should be designed and what kinds of knowledge and evidence are required to assemble it. As noted in Chapter 1, however, in the pursuit of better policies, a greater emphasis on the improved design of tool mixes has been a feature of policy design research over the past decade, and these studies have increased awareness of the many dilemmas that can appear in the path of effective policy tool or 'toolkit' designs and policy-making realities.

As we have seen, mixes are combinations of policy instruments that are expected to achieve particular policy objectives and which are generally seen as more efficient and effective than single instrument uses (Gunningham et al. 1998). Good policy designs are expected to feature mixes in which there are few contradictions and to result from a logical effort to match policy tools and goals based on theory and experience.

In assembling such designs, an intimate knowledge of the strengths and weaknesses of individual tools is required along with an idea of how they fit together and operate in a mix. Some instruments may work well with others by nature – as is the case with 'self-regulation' set within a regulatory compliance framework, for example (Grabosky 1995) – while other combinations may not, such as, notably, independently developed subsidies and regulation which often contradict each other and provide mixed signals to targets. Other mixes may also have evolved in a certain way which has undermined, or improved, their effectiveness, while others may have never been very effective in the first place and remain so.

Concerns about how to make the most of policy synergies while curtailing contradictions in the formulation of new or reformed policy packages have been a major topic of investigation within the design orientation in policy studies (Hou and Brewer 2010; Howlett and Muhkerjee 2019). As we have seen, a major concern of those working in contemporary policy design studies has been the process of policy improvement: determining whether reform of combinations of different policy instruments which have evolved independently and incrementally can accomplish complex policy goals as effectively as more deliberately customized portfolios and taking action accordingly in the form of the elaboration and implementation of policy 'patches' (Howlett 2014).

Principles of effective policy designs based on the character of tools

This literature on policy design has highlighted several key principles for effective policy designs based on the 'character' or innate characteristics of the tools set out in Chapters 3–6 and of mixes based upon them. These principles can inform policy design considerations in this area. Seven of these principles are listed in the following sections while other principles linked more closely to the nature of the policy design context are elaborated afterwards.

Parsimonious tool use and the Tinbergen rule

The older literature on policy design suggested several maxims or heuristics which can be used to head off common errors in policy design. The first and oldest of these is to observe parsimony in tool selection.

An oft-cited rule in this area, for example, is that the optimal ratio of the number of tools to goals is 1:1 (Knudson 2009), an axiom first put forward by Tinbergen (1952) who argued that the number of policy tools in any mix should roughly match the number of goals or objectives set for the policy. This is a reasonable rule-of-thumb for designers, for which Tinbergen provides some logical justification in his discussion of information and administrative costs associated with redundant tools in the area of economic policy. Assuming that utilizing more instruments costs less than utilizing fewer, and that redundancy is not a virtue, this maxim translates easily enough into a basic efficiency principle for policy mixes.

Maximizing complementary effects and minimizing counterproductive ones

Most observers, however, including Tinbergen, were and are well aware that combinations of tools are typically used to address a policy goal, not a single instrument. As Tinbergen (1952: 37) himself argued, 'a priori there is no guarantee that the number of targets always equals the number of instruments', and (71) 'it goes without saying that complicated systems of economic policy (for example) will almost invariably be a mixture of instruments'.

Assuming most policies will be a mix of tools, a major issue for both scholars and practitioners is tied to the fact that not all of the tools involved and invoked in a mix are inherently complementary (Boonekamp 2006) in the sense that they may evoke contradictory responses from policy targets. Some combinations, of course, may be more virtuous in providing a reinforcing or supplementing arrangement (Hou and Brewer 2010). And some other arrangements may also be unnecessarily duplicative, while in others some redundancy may be advantageous (Braathen 2007).

A key principle of current policy design thinking is to try to maximize supplementary effects while minimizing counterproductive ones. 'Smart' design implies creating packages which take these precepts into account in their formulation or packaging (Gunningham et al. 1998).

Although a consensus does not exist on the terms and definitions of all the possible conflicts, complementarities and synergies between different tools and types of instruments (Oikonomou and Jepma 2008; Oikonomou et al. 2011) it can be argued that the types of interaction found between tools will vary such that in some cases there will be:

1 a strong conflict where the addition of an instrument (X) leads to a reduction of the effect of a second instrument (Y) in the combination: 0 < X+Y < 1,
2 a weak conflict (partial complementarity) where the addition of one instrument to another leads to a positive effect on the combination, but lower than the one that would take place if both were used separately: 1 < X+Y < 2,
3 a situation of full complementarity where X adds fully to the effect of Y in the combination: X+Y = 2
4 a situation of synergy where adding X to Y magnifies the impact of the combination: X+Y > 2 (del Río 2014).

Such interactions can range from 'no effect' to 'direct interaction', with effects ranging from 'duplication' (positive or negative redundancy) to 'extended coverage' (positive redundancy) (del Rio 2014). Effective design involves avoiding strong conflicts, minimizing weak ones and promoting complementarity and synergies. While this becomes more difficult to do as the level of complexity of the design space increases, it remains a central goal of policy portfolio design.

Sequencing: moving up the scale of coercion in instrument choices

If policies are to entail a mix of tools, however, this raises the question of whether they should all be adopted at one time or *sequenced* in some fashion. A third principle of policy design which can be derived from the older literature on the subject addresses these issues. This is the idea that governments should be parsimonious in not only the number of instruments chosen at a specific point in time to attain a goal, but also dynamically or sequentially. In the mid-1970s and the early 1980s, for example, G. Bruce Doern and his colleagues argued not only that different policy instruments varied primarily in terms of the 'degree of government coercion' each instrument choice entailed (Doern and Wilson 1974) but also that tool choices should only 'move up the spectrum' of coercion from minimum towards maximum, if and when necessary.

This rationale is again based on a cost–effort calculation and is also linked to an appreciation of the ideological preferences of liberal-democratic governments for limited state activity and upon recognition of the difficulties posed to the exercise of state power and policy compliance by the relative political 'strength' of the societal actors and their ability to resist government efforts to shape their behaviour. Assuming that all instruments are more or less technically 'substitutable' or could perform any task – although not necessarily as easily or at the same cost – Doern and his colleagues argued that in a liberal democratic society, governments, for both cost and ideological reasons, prefer to use the least coercive instruments available and only 'move up the scale' of coercion as far as is necessary in order to overcome societal resistance to attaining their goals (Howlett 1991). Preferring 'self-regulation' as a basic default, for example, they argued governments should first attempt to influence overall target group performance through exhortation and then only add instruments as required in order to compel recalcitrant societal actors to abide by their wishes, eventually culminating, if necessary, in the fully public provision of goods and services.

Utilize coherence, consistency and congruence as measures of the design integrity and superiority of a mix

Much work on policy design and policy mixes has also focused on the need for the various parts of a mix or portfolio to be *integrated* for maximum effectiveness (Briassoulis 2005). Policies are composed of several elements, and some correspondence across these elements is required if policy goals are to be integrated successfully with policy means. Measures of integration highlighted in the literature include criteria such as '*consistency*' (the ability of multiple policy tools to reinforce rather than undermine each other in the pursuit of policy goals), '*coherence*' (or the ability of multiple policy goals to coexist with each other and with instrument norms in a logical fashion, the relationships within the shaded area in figure) and '*congruence*' (or the ability of goals and instruments to work together in a uni-directional or mutually supportive fashion) as important measures of optimality in policy mixes following this integrative logic (Kern and Howlett 2009; Lanzalaco 2011).

That is, as del Rio (2009) has argued, design principles to promote integration in complex mixes require a broader view of the elements found in policy mixes than is typically found in the literature on the subject. Appropriate policy evaluation, appraisal and design cannot be conducted in a narrow context. The focus should not be on the functioning of specific instruments with respect to a single criterion, but rather upon the functioning of the whole policy mix and the conflicts and synergies that exist with respect to multiple goals and criteria within it.

This is a particular challenge in situations featuring overlapping policies and governments. What might be regarded as conflictive in the interactions within an instrument mix might not be so problematic when a broader picture of multiple policies or governments is considered and vice-versa. That is, there is an issue of both horizontal and vertical coordination involved in tool mix design in the sense that tools and goals may conflict not only at one level of government but also within policy regimes when these have, as they commonly do, a multi-level aspect (Howlett and del Rio 2015). The existence of different goals at different administrative levels complicates vertical coordination and integration. Different benefits and costs for different constituencies stemming from supranational policies or the existence of federal governmental arrangements, for example, may complicate considerations of political feasibility and different goals may create winners and losers at different administrative levels and lead to unacceptable distributional effects. All of these factors must enter into design considerations.

Avoiding over- and under-designing

Prima facie, simple Tinbergen-type single instrument, single-goal, single-policy, single-government instrument mixes represent only one of many possible types of instrument mixes. And this means that the standard Tinbergen design maxim of 'one goal – one tool' proposed as a suitable design maxim to address the issue of instrument optimality is unlikely to be put into practice very often, and other principles need to be developed to take its place within more complex designs.

The recent literature on 'disproportionality' in government responses to problems is very useful in this regard (Maor 2017). As discussed in Chapter 2 Governments often over- and under-react to the actual severity of problems, sometimes intentionally for political or electoral purposes (for example, to be seen as being tough on crime) or unintentionally (not accurately foreseeing the threat of an epidemic, for example). Both situations lead to over- and under-designing and are generally to be avoided (Maor 2017).

This means utilizing not only the number of tools required to reasonably attain policy goals and achieve compliance with government wishes and no more than that, but also to seriously consider a 'fudge factor' or needed level of redundancy in order to deal with unforeseen or under-estimated problems. While it may not be clear at the start what the 'correct' number is and how large a factor to allocate, beginning with a smaller number and adding tools as needed to ensure compliance and monitoring the impact and effect of each additional tool can help identify it while avoiding tendencies to over design or over-react to immediate circumstances and exigencies.

Better matching tools and target behaviours in compliance regimes

There also is a significant behavioural component to the design of policy mixes, which is critical to policy success and failure. That is, as discussed in Chapter 2, it is critically important for policy-making that the behaviour resulting from policy activity and the implementation of policy tools and expenditure of governing resources matches that anticipated prior to deployment (Duesberg et al. 2014).

Policy tool use and behavioural expectations are linked in the sense that the use of policy tools involves implicit or explicit assumptions and expectations about the effect tool deployment will have upon those impacted by it whether this involves, as set out in Chapter 6, "system 1" automatic responses or 'system 2' deliberative ones. In most cases, with the exception of those symbolic instances where 'over-design' is welcomed, such as in areas of national security or crime prevention, efficient policy designs are those that affect only those targets whose behaviour it is necessary to change and with only the minimum necessary levels of coercion, expenditure and display.

Policy designs themselves, however, have often been developed with only the most rudimentary and cursory knowledge of how those expected to be affected by an instrument are, in fact, likely to react to it. Regardless of whether those targets are purely social constructions with few empirical referents or if they reflect more objective assessment of the actual behaviour of relevant groups of policy actors, however, it is critical for effective policy-making that actual target behaviour matches expectations, and behavioural research is thus a key aspect of effective policy design (Nielsen and Parker 2012).

Designing and assessing policy prototypes through experiments and pilot projects

The use of pilot projects and careful evaluation of target nature and compliance regimes is critical here (Weaver 2014). The development of pilot projects or policy experiments in which new designs and ideas are tried out and proven prior to their being 'scaled up' or 'scaled down' and put into widespread practice can be very useful in determining and estimating the behavioural changes caused by policy tools and designs.

Such policy experimentation can be used to pre-test different programmes and policies for their likely impacts, process of implementation and stakeholder acceptability prior to launching these fully or on a large scale.

Policy pilots form a common and important form of policy experimentation and involve the introduction of major government policies or programmes at a 'controlled small-scale' or phased manner, allowing them to be tested, evaluated and adjusted before being rolled out jurisdiction-wide. Planning 'well-designed pilots' alongside a fully functioning policy can help test a policy's performance along with identification of emerging issues and help inform any necessary policy adjustments (Swanson et al. 2010).

Pilots aid in policy appraisal and provide useful insights for dealing with complex policy issues amid conditions of high uncertainty (Vreugdenhil et al. 2012). The small-scale and experimental nature of pilots can encourage policy innovations, and policy-makers should, and do, consider pilot projects and other forms of policy experiments in order to test new policy and programme approaches (Nair and Howlett 2016).

Principles of policy design based on the design context

While knowledge of the character of individual tools and mixes is important in developing principles for policy design, understanding the policy design *context* is equally so (deLeon 1988). Kirschen et al. (1964), for example, noted very early on that the key determinants of the policy choices examined in their pioneering study of post-WWII European economic policy were the economic objective pursued *and* the structural and conjunctural context of the choice. While the choice of a specific instrument could be made on essentially technical grounds, according to criteria such as efficiency, cost or effectiveness, they found it was also affected by the political preferences of interest groups and governments, and a variety of sociological and ideological constraints which would also inform tool choices and preferences (238–44). The US pioneer of policy studies, Harold Lasswell (1954), too, noted that the extent to which governments could affect every aspect of policy-making through design manipulations varied depending upon the circumstances and actors involved in any given context and argued that a principal task of the policy sciences must be to understand the nuances of these situations and calibrate their actions and their effects accordingly.

Lasswell also noted that this design context has a temporal as well as a spatial dimension, since many regimes have developed haphazardly over time. That is, across time periods, new instruments appear and old ones may have evolved or been eliminated. How the processes of policy formulation followed in adopting such complex designs have unfolded and how this has affected policy goals and instrument logics is a subject of much interest in the design world (Larsen et al. 2006).

As set out in earlier Chapters, the existing evidence shows that suboptimal or poorly integrated situations are very common in many existing mixes which have developed through processes of policy layering and stretching (Miller 1990; Bode 2006). These kinds of 'unintentional' mixes can be contrasted with 'smarter' designs or 'packages' which involve creating new sets of tools specifically intended to overcome or avoid the problems associated with layering but which may be difficult to put into practice. All these processes and change dynamics again focus attention on the need to properly sequence instrument choices within mixes (Taeihagh et al. 2013).

Many existing studies assume, whether explicitly or implicitly, that *any* combination of tools is possible in *any* circumstance. That is, that decision-makers have unlimited *degrees of freedom* in their design choices. Empirical studies, however, have noted that this kind of freedom in combining design elements is to be found only in very specific circumstances – either development of a new portfolio in a new area of concern, such as social media or internet related activity in the present era, or what Kathleen Thelen (2003) has termed 'replacement' or 'exhaustion' when older tool elements have been swept aside or abandoned and a new mix can be designed or adopted *de novo*. Most existing mixes or portfolios instead have emerged from a gradual historical process in which a policy mix has slowly built up over time through processes of incremental change or successive reformulation or 'layering' which heavily impacts what can be done to alter or amend an existing instrument mix (Capano 2019). This insight generates a second set of maxims concerning effective policy design in these different design contexts.

Promoting patching as well as packaging in portfolio design

As we have seen in earlier chapters, at least two distinct design techniques emerge from formulation efforts which may take the form of policy 'packaging', that is the creation of new mixes or the more common form of 'patching' in which only selected aspects of existing mixes are altered.

Recognizing the drawbacks of layering, conversion and drift as often promoting unintentional and poorly integrated mixes, many critics have increasingly argued for the promotion of complex policy mixes through replacement. However, multiple policy tool portfolios which have evolved over a long period time through processes of incremental layering, often cannot easily be replaced. Policy 'patching' is a more realistic design modality in such contexts and, if done properly, with a clear eye on promoting coherence and integration in complex environments can achieve complex and ambitious policy goals in as efficient and effective a way as those designs which are consciously created as interlocking packages of measures (Howlett and Rayner 2013).

Goodness of fit: the need for designs to match governance mode and policy regime capacities

It is also the case that design choices emerge from and must generally be congruent with the governance modes or styles practiced in particular jurisdictions and sectors. *Goodness of fit* between tool and context is thus a key concern in contemporary policy design considerations and can be seen to occur at several different levels (Brandl 1988).

That is, different orientations towards state activity require different capabilities on the part of state and societal actors, and different governance modes and styles constrain alternatives in certain ways, promoting 'favorite' or preferred sets of tools such as, for example, a preference for regulation over direct provision as exists in the United States or, until recently, the opposite predilection in the case of many European countries (Howlett and Tosun 2019). Similarly, planning and 'steering' involve direct coordination of key actors by governments, requiring a high level of government policy capacity to identify and utilize a wide range of policy tools in a successful policy 'mix' or 'arrangement' which a government may not possess. This can lead to specific kinds of preferences for particular kinds of tools which make the design and adoption of policy packages simpler, less costly and less time-consuming than might otherwise be the case (Howlett and Rayner 2013).

Policy designs must take into account both the desired governance context and the actual resources available to a governmental or non-governmental actor in carrying out its appointed role.

Degrees of freedom in policy designs: matching policy designing and policy designs over time

Third, as noted earlier, empirical studies in many policy areas have shown that many existing policy mixes were not 'designed' in the classical sense of conscious, intentional and deliberate planning according to well-established or oft-used governance principles but rather evolved or were developed through a non-design process in the first place, or both. As Christensen et al. (2002) have argued, the issue here then becomes the leeway or degrees of freedom policy designers have in developing *new* designs, given existing historical arrangements, path dependencies, policy legacies and lock-in effects.

That is, in addition to the requirements of 'goodness of fit' with prevailing governance modes with respect to the logic of policy design, there are also constraints imposed on designs by existing trajectories of policy development. As Christensen et al. note, 'these factors place constraints on and create opportunities for purposeful choice, deliberate instrumental actions and intentional efforts taken by political and administrative leaders to launch administrative reforms through administrative design' (2002: 158). Determining how much room to manoeuvre or degrees of freedom designers have to be creative (Considine 2012) or, to put it another way, to what degree they are 'context bound' in time and space (Howlett 2011), is a key for contemporary design studies.

Conclusion: designing for resilience and robustness

These principles around instrument mix content and context provide some instruction and serve as rules of thumb which can help guide policy-makers to choose 'the right tool for the job'. But there is always, as Simon noted, some uncertainty around the future, and policy-makers and designers must be ready to deal with these unknowns. As the discussion in Chapter 2 highlighted, there is often a high level of knowledge and other kinds of uncertainty in policy-making, and the modern policy studies movement began with the observation that public policy-making not only commonly results from the interactions of policy-makers in the exercise of power rather than knowledge, and also with the recognition that this does not always guarantee effective policies or the attainment of desired results. Even in cases of well-thought-out and intentioned or otherwise well-designed policies, failures commonly occur over time. That is, even when policies are designed with a clear evidentiary basis in a model process, they may still fail if they do not adapt to changings circumstances and concerns, as policy implementation proceeds and the policy is put into action (Nair and Howlett 2017).

The modern policy sciences are founded on the idea that accumulating and utilizing knowledge of the effects and impacts of a relatively well-known set of policy means developed through analysis and experience over many years of state-building activity can more effectively marshal and utilize them than is likely to occur with purely power-driven non-design processes in highly uncertain policy contexts.

Studies of policy uncertainty and policy failure have emphasized the need to have policies able to improvise in the face of an uncertain future, meaning there is a need to design and adopt policies featuring agility, improvisation and flexibility, that is, designs which feature *robustness* over many circumstances and are *resilient* in the face of challenges (Capano and Woo 2018).

By definition, these kinds of designs require redundant resources and capabilities, and this need is in strong opposition to ideas about design which equate better designs solely with efficiency and the allocation of the minimum amount of resources, and to those which only emphasize routinization and the replication of standard operating procedures and programme elements. While these latter designs may be appropriate in some circumstances where competition from other service providers might provide a degree of system-level resilience and/or in well-known or stable environments where surprise is unlikely, this is not true in many public sector activities where government is the sole provider of particular goods and services and future scenarios are unknown, contested or unpredictable.

As studies of crisis management and other similar situations have emphasized, in these instances, robustness is needed and can be planned for (Moynihan 2008). Similarly, the need to develop policies which can address long-term issues such as climate change in the face of shorter-term partisan, electoral and budgetary challenges, amongst others, has raised to the forefront the need to design policy mixes which are 'sticky' or resilient in the face of new or mounting challenges (Jordan and Matt 2014).

Studies of policy uncertainty, crisis management, policy learning and policy capacity, for example, have all emphasized the need to design some modicum of redundancy into most policies. This means to design policies capable of maintaining the same performance in the face of any type of internal/external perturbation in order to deal with surprise and avoid policy failure caused by unexpected or unknown occurrences which upset initial design specifications and assumptions.

On a substantive level, 'robust' policies are those which incorporate some slack, allowing room for adjustments as conditions change. Robust policies, as in the case of a bridge or building, need to be 'overdesigned' or 'over-engineered' in order to allow for a greater range of effective, thus 'robust', responses across contexts and time. This can be effective and even efficient over the long-term, for example, in the case of 'automatic stabilizers' such as welfare payments or unemployment insurance payments which maintain some level of spending and saving despite a general economic contraction and remove some funds from investment availability during boom times. Organizations can become too lean and may eliminate elements that could be useful when circumstances change, thus restricting the ability of an organization to respond to surprises. The ability to alter and adapt policies on the fly – to improvise effectively – also requires some level of redundancy in procedural tools and components of policy mixes.

That is, these circumstances require not just robust policies but also policy mixes that utilize procedural implementation tools to promote *resilience*. Maintaining policy robustness in such circumstances requires a style of decision-making which allows response to surprises to be improvised and implemented in an effective way *as they occur* (Room 2013). Having procedural tools such as built-in policy reviews, and mechanisms for outside evaluation and control including provisions for future public hearings and information access, disclosure and dissemination (Lang 2016) allow more significant adjustments to changing circumstances to occur as policy implementation unfolds and are key elements that need to be incorporated in any policy design expected to last more than a few years.

References

Bode, I. "Disorganized Welfare Mixes: Voluntary Agencies and New Governance Regimes in Western Europe." *Journal of European Social Policy* 16, no. 4 (2006): 346–59.

Boonekamp, Piet G.M. "Actual Interaction Effects Between Policy Measures for Energy Efficiency—A Qualitative Matrix Method and Quantitative Simulation Results for Households." *Energy* 31, no. 14 (November 2006): 2848–73.

Braathen, Nils Axel. "Instrument Mixes for Environmental Policy: How Many Stones Should Be Used to Kill a Bird?" *International Review of Environmental and Resource Economics* 1, no. 2 (May 16, 2007): 185–235.

Brandl, James. "On Politics and Policy Analysis as the Design and Assessment of Institutions." *Journal of Policy Analysis and Management* 7, no. 3 (1988): 419–24.

Briassoulis, H. "Complex Environment Problems and the Quest of Policy Integration." In *Policy Integration for Complex Environmental Problems: The Example of Mediterranean Desertification*, edited by Briassoulis, H, 1–49. Aldershot: Ashgate, 2005.

Capano, Giliberto. "Reconceptualizing Layering. From Mode of Institutional Change to Mode of Institutional Design: Types and Outputs." *Public Administration*, forthcoming 2019. doi:10.1111/padm.12583.

Capano, Giliberto, and Jun Jie Woo. "Resilience and Robustness in Policy Design: A Critical Appraisal." *Policy Sciences* 37, no. 4 (2018): 422–40.

Christensen, T., P. Laegreid, and L. R. Wise. "Transforming Administrative Policy." *Public Administration* 80, no. 1 (2002): 153–79.

Considine, Mark. "Thinking Outside the Box? Applying Design Theory to Public Policy." *Politics & Policy* 40, no. 4 (2012): 704–24.

deLeon, Peter. "The Contextual Burdens of Policy Design." *Policy Studies Journal* 17, no. 2 (1988): 297–309.

Doern, G. B., and V. S. Wilson. "Conclusions and Observations." In *Issues in Canadian Public Policy*, edited by Doern, G. B., and V. S. Wilson, 337–45. Toronto, ON: Macmillan, 1974.

Duesberg, Stefanie, Áine Ní Dhubháin, and Deirdre O'Connor. "Assessing Policy Tools for Encouraging Farm Afforestation in Ireland." *Land Use Policy* 38 (May 2014): 194–203.

Gleeson, Deborah, David Legge, Deirdre O'Neill, and Monica Pfeffer. "Negotiating Tensions in Developing Organizational Policy Capacity: Comparative Lessons to Be Drawn." *Journal of Comparative Policy Analysis: Research and Practice* 13, no. 3 (June 2011): 237–63.

Grabosky, P. "Counterproductive Regulation." *International Journal of the Sociology of Law* 23 (1995): 347–69.

Gunningham, N., P. Grabosky, and D. Sinclair. *Smart Regulation: Designing Environmental Policy*. Oxford: Clarendon Press, 1998.

Head, Brian W. "Toward More 'Evidence-Informed' Policy Making?" *Public Administration Review* 76, no. 3 (May 1, 2016): 472–84.

Hou, Yilin, and Gene Brewer. "Substitution and Supplementation Between Co- Functional Policy Instruments: Evidence from State Budget Stabilization Practices." *Public Administration Review* 70, no. 6 (2010): 914–24.

Howlett, M. "Policy Instruments, Policy Styles, and Policy Implementation: National Approaches to Theories of Instrument Choice." *Policy Studies Journal* 19, no. 2 (1991): 1–21.

Howlett, M. *Designing Public Policies: Principles and Instruments*. New York: Routledge, 2011.

Howlett, M. "From the 'Old' to the 'New' Policy Design: Design Thinking Beyond Markets and Collaborative Governance." *Policy Sciences* 47, no. 33 (May 28, 2014): 187–207.

Howlett, Michael P., and Jeremy Rayner. "Patching vs Packaging: Complementary Effects, Goodness of Fit, Degrees of Freedom and Intentionality in Policy Portfolio Design." SSRN Scholarly Paper. Rochester, NY: Social Science Research Network, 2013.

Howlett, Michael, and Pablo del Rio. "The Parameters of Policy Portfolios: Verticality and Horizontality in Design Spaces and Their Consequences for Policy Mix Formulation." *Environment and Planning C* 33, no. 5 (2015): 1233–45.

Howlett, Michael, and Ishani Mukherjee. *Handbook of Policy Design*. New York: Routledge, 2019.

Howlett, Michael, and Jale Tosun, eds. *Policy Styles and Policy-Making: Exploring the Linkages*. London: Routledge, 2019.

Jordan, Andrew, and Elah Matt. "Designing Policies That Intentionally Stick: Policy Feedback in a Changing Climate." *Policy Sciences* 47, no. 3 (2014): 227–47

Kern, Florian, and Michael Howlett. "Implementing Transition Management as Policy Reforms: A Case Study of the Dutch Energy Sector." *Policy Sciences* 42, no. 4 (November 1, 2009): 391–408.

Kirschen, E. S., J. Benard, H. Besters, F. Blackaby, O. Eckstein, J. Faaland, F. Hartog, L. Morissens, and E. Tosco. *Economic Policy in Our Time*. Chicago, IL: Rand McNally, 1964.

Knudson, William A. "The Environment, Energy, and the Tinbergen Rule." *Bulletin of Science, Technology & Society* 29, no. 4 (August 1, 2009): 308–12.

Lang, Achim. "Collaborative Governance in Health and Technology Policy: The Use and Effects of Procedural Policy Instruments." *Administration & Society*, forthcoming (August 10, 2016).

Lanzalaco, Luca. "Bringing the Olympic Rationality Back In? Coherence, Integration and Effectiveness of Public Policies." *World Political Science Review* 7, no. 1 (May 25, 2011): 1098.

Larsen, T. P., P. Taylor-Gooby, and J. Kananen. "New Labour's Policy Style: A Mix of Policy Approaches." *International Social Policy* 35, no. 4 (2006): 629–49.

Lasswell, H. "Key Symbols, Signs and Icons." In *Symbols and Values: An Initial Study*, edited by L. Bryson, L. Finkelstein, R. M. MacIver, and Richard McKean, 77–94. New York: Harper and Brothers, 1954.

Maor, Moshe. "The Implications of the Emerging Disproportionate Policy Perspective for the New Policy Design Studies." *Policy Sciences* 50, no. 3 (September 1, 2017): 383–98.

Miller, S. M. "The Evolving Welfare State Mixes." In *Shifts in the Welfare Mix: Their Impact on Work, Social Services and Welfare Policies*, edited by A. Evers and H. Winterberger, 371–88. Frankfurt: Campus Verlag, 1990.

Moynihan, Donald P. "Combining Structural Forms in the Search for Policy Tools: Incident Command Systems in U.S. Crisis Management." *Governance* 21, no. 2 (2008): 205–29.

Nair, Sreeja, and Michael Howlett. "Policy Myopia as a Source of Policy Failure: Adaptation and Policy Learning under Deep Uncertainty." *Policy & Politics* 45, no. 1 (2017): 103–18.

Nair, Sreeja, and Michael Howlett. "Meaning and Power in the Design and Development of Policy Experiments." *Futures*, Policy-making for the long term: puzzling and powering to navigate wicked futures issues, 76 (February 2016): 67–74.

Nielsen, Vibeke Lehmann, and Christine Parker. "Mixed Motives: Economic, Social, and Normative Motivations in Business Compliance." *Law & Policy* 34, no. 4 (2012): 428–62.

Oikonomou, V., A. Flamos, D. Zeugolis, and S. Grafakos. "A Qualitative Assessment of EU Energy Policy Interactions." *Energy Sources, Part B: Economics, Planning, and Policy* 7, no. 2 (2011): 177–87.

Oikonomou, V., and C. J. Jepma. "A Framework on Interactions of Climate and Energy Policy Instruments." *Mitigation and Adaptation Strategies for Global Change* 13, no. 2 (February 15, 2008): 131–56.

Riddell, Norman. *Policy Research Capacity in the Federal Government.* Ottawa, ON: Policy Research Initiative, 1998.

Rio, Pablo del. "Interactions between Climate and Energy Policies: The Case of Spain." *Climate Policy* 9, no. 2 (2009): 119–38.

Rio, Pablo del. "On Evaluating Success in Complex Policy Mixes: The Case of Renewable Energy Support Schemes." *Policy Sciences* 47, no. 3 (2014): 267–87.

Room, Graham. "Evidence for Agile Policy Makers: The Contribution of Transformative Realism." *Evidence & Policy: A Journal of Research, Debate and Practice* 9, no. 2 (May 24, 2013): 225–44.

Sanderson, I. "Evaluation, Policy Learning and Evidence-Based Policy Making." *Public Administration* 80, no. 1 (2002): 1–22.

Schon, Donald A. *The Reflective Practitioner: How Professionals Think In Action.* New York: Basic Books, 1984.

Swanson, Darren, Stephan Barg, Stephen Tyler, Henry Venema, Sanjay Tomar, Suruchi Bhadwal, Sreeja Nair, Dimple Roy, and John Drexhage. "Seven Tools for Creating Adaptive Policies." *Technological Forecasting and Social Change* 77, no. 6 (2010): 924–39.

Taeihagh, Araz, Moshe Givoni, and René Bañares-Alcántara. "Which Policy First? A Network-Centric Approach for the Analysis and Ranking of Policy Measures." *Environment and Planning B: Planning and Design* 40, no. 4 (2013): 595–616.

Thelen, K. "How Institutions Evolve: Insights from Comparative Historical Analysis." In *Comparative Historical Analysis in the Social Sciences*, edited by J. Mahoney and D. Rueschemeyer, 208–40. Cambridge: Cambridge University Press, 2003.

Tinbergen, Jan. *On the Theory of Economic Policy.* Dordrecht: North-Holland Pub. Co., 1952.

Vreugdenhil, Heleen, Susan Taljaard, and Jill H. Slinger. "Pilot Projects and Their Diffusion: A Case Study of Integrated Coastal Management in South Africa." *International Journal of Sustainable Development* 15, no. 1/2 (2012): 148.

Weaver, R. Kent. "Compliance Regimes and Barriers to Behavioral Change." *Governance* 27, no. 2 (April 1, 2014): 243–65.

Index

Note: **Bold** page numbers refers to tables and *italics* page numbers refer to figures.

Made in United States
North Haven, CT
08 January 2024

47200244R00085